D1363676

A Theory of Political Integration

THE DORSEY SERIES IN POLITICAL SCIENCE

EDITOR **NORTON E. LONG** *Brandeis University*

A Theory of

Political

Integration

By CLAUDE AKE
Columbia University

1967: THE DORSEY PRESS

Homewood, Illinois

First Printing, September, 1967

Library of Congress Catalog Card No. 67–30065

Printed in the United States of America

To the Social Engineers
of the New States
Who Know the Frustrations
And the Excitement of
Becoming.

Acknowledgments

I have for a long time anticipated with pleasure the opportunity of returning thanks that are due.

I am deeply indebted to Professors Herbert A. Deane, L. Gray Cowan, and Immanuel Wallerstein under whose tutelage this quest began; their guidance and understanding were assets of incalcuable value. I am grateful to Professor Terence Hopkins whose incisive criticisms of an earlier draft of the manuscript saved me from many errors of fact and judgment and to Professor Maurice Goldsmith for his witty and sobering comments on some parts of the manuscript.

It is a duty and a pleasure to acknowledge my indebtedness to my colleagues at Columbia, especially Anthony Berret, Katherine P. Moseley, and Michael Ross for tolerating my tiresome obsession with political integration and for helping me clarify my ideas. Special thanks are due to Catherine Bodard for her helpful suggestions and encouragement.

My indebtedness to other writers on this intricate subject is embarrassing; my obligations to them are much greater than my references in the text suggest. Scholarship is indeed a collective enterprise.

I wish to express my deep appreciation to the Rockefeller Foundation for making it possible for me to study in the United States. The Editors of *World Politics* and *Comparative Studies in Society and History* kindly permitted me to use material I had published in their pages. I thank them.

New York City   CLAUDE AKE
September, 1967

Table of Contents

Chapter 1

Introduction

This study develops from an analysis of the problem of political integration in the new states to the more general question of the capacity of political systems for undertaking social change on a large scale and for withstanding the disruptive impact of such change. It attempts to formulate a theory of the conditions of political integration, engineered large-scale social change, and political stability and of the relation between the three phenomena.

The problem of political integration is a shorthand for two related problems:

a) How to elicit from subjects deference and devotion to the claims of the state.

b) How to increase normative consensus governing political behavior among members of the political system.

In essence the problem of political integration is one of developing a political culture and of inducing commitment to it. Political culture "consists of the system of empirical beliefs, expressive symbols and values which defines the situation in which political action takes place."[1] For the individual the political culture

---

[1]Sidney Verba, "Comparative Political Culture," in Lucian Pye and Sidney Verba (eds.), *Political Culture and Political Development* (Princeton, N.J.: Princeton University Press, 1965), p. 513.

provides the guidelines of political behavior. For the political system as a whole, the political culture provides "a systematic structure of values and rational considerations which ensures coherence in the performance of institutions and organizations."[2]

Some points about the concept of political culture should be underlined. First, the beliefs—such as belief about the trustworthiness of other members of the society—which are relevant to the concept of political culture are not so because they are uniquely political in nature but only because they affect political behavior in an important way. The political culture is not different from the general culture of the society; it is merely an aspect of it. That political culture is only an aspect of the general culture does not warrant the conclusion that the concept is superfluous or that it is analytically useless. To insist that one must always talk of culture rather than political culture because the former subsumes the latter is as absurd as insisting that the distinction between economy and industry is useless because industry is a part of the economy. To be sure, the degree of cultural homogeneity is the most important determinant of the level of political integration (essentially the degree of normative consensus about political behavior). However it is possible for a political system to achieve a level of integration quite out of proportion to its cultural homogeneity. The degree of normative consensus may vary from one sphere of activity to another in the same society, and the sharedness of values in certain spheres of activity may, depending on what the values are that are shared, exacerbate conflict or inhibit consensus in certain other spheres of activity.

Second, we cannot deduce a high degree of political

---

[2]Lucian Pye, "Political Culture and Political Development," in Pye and Verba (eds.), *op. cit.*, p. 7.

integration from the mere fact of the existence of commonly held political beliefs without inquiring into the nature of these beliefs. To use Verba's example, the belief that political power ought to be used to promote the interest of "a parochially defined group" may be commonly held. But the fact that members of the political system may differ on the particular parochial group whose interest is to be promoted may lead to grave political strife.[3] The nature of the values which constitute the political culture must be such that commitment to them furthers the persistence of the political structure.

One important element in the political culture is the individual's belief about the ultimate focus of his political identity. All other things being equal, to the extent that the citizens of the state identify with it, to the extent that they believe that it deserves their loyalty, their propensity to defer to the claims of the state is increased. It is now easier to see the relation between the two problems we have synthesized as the problem of political integration. The first problem is a subdivision of the second in the sense that the belief that the state deserves their loyalty is one of the essential values that political actors must internalize if the political system is to be highly integrated. While the two problems are related, they are not identical. Deference to the claims of the state does not imply normative consensus; it could issue from coercion.

A political system is integrated to the extent that the minimal units (individual political actors) develop in the course of political interaction a pool of commonly accepted norms regarding political behavior and a commitment to the political behavior patterns legitimized by these norms. Commitment to these norms channels

---

[3]Sidney Verba, in Pye and Verba, *op. cit.,* p. 526.

the flow of exchanges (outputs and inputs, actions and reactions, expectations and responses) among interacting political actors. In effect, it gives coherence and predictability to political life. A political system is malintegrated to the extent that political exchanges are not regulated by a normative culture. In malintegrated political systems the emphasis is on effective rather than on legitimate means for pursuing political goals; in highly integrated political systems the emphasis is on legitimate rather than on effective means.

Regularity in the flow of exchanges is conceivable in the political system whose members do not share a common value orientation. Indeed, if regularity were completely absent, we could not properly talk of a political system. But what regularity exists in this case comes largely from coercion.

It is clear that what makes a political system integrated is not the very fact of the predictability of the flow of exchanges. If this predictability derives exclusively from nonlegitimate coercion, the political system is not strictly speaking integrated—we may say that it is integrated in a minimal sense (i.e., held together "physically")—even when such coercion is effective enough to ensure that the main structural features of the political system persist. In a minimally integrated political system—and such a political system can only be an ideal type—the "subjects"[4] obey the rulers not out of a sense of obligation but only because they are obliged to. I am inclined to think that a minimally integrated political system is potentially unstable. So long as obedience is not transformed into duty, might into right, rebellion

---

[4] I use subject advisedly because such a system of relations is strictly speaking precivil. Some people will be subordinated to others merely because of a differential distribution of "strengths."

is endemic. Perhaps, I should add that the political system held together purely by normative consensus (what we may call optimal integration) is also an ideal type. We know of no political system that does not employ legitimate coercion in some form or other.

The view of political integration taken here leans towards the consensus theory of social integration. The consensus theory sees value consensus as the pervasive character of society. On this view the role of coercion in social integration is the subordinate one of controlling deviancy. The difficulties of the consensus theory are now familiar knowledge. Invariably the consensus theorist finds himself in the rather uncomfortable position of explaining all antisocial behavior as deviancy which is in turn explained in terms of role strain, normative dissensus, and imperfections of the socialization process. If the consensus theory is right in representing all antisocial behavior as essentially imperfections (e.g., the undersocialization of the deviant) in the mechanisms of the social system, then there is no reason why we cannot by an ingenious feat of social engineering realize the anarchist utopia of unregulated social harmony.

The consensus theory has had to compete with the coercion theory, a view of social integration that can be traced as far back as Hobbes and even beyond. Contemporary coercion theorists such as Dahrendorf argue that the consensus theory grossly underestimates the importance of force in integration in that far from depending on value consensus, social cohesion depends on "force and constraint on the domination of some and the subjection of others."[5]

It seems to me that it is a mistake to oppose the

---

[5]Ralf Dahrendorf, *Class and Class Conflict in Industrial Society* (Stanford, Calif.: Stanford University Press, 1959) , p. 157.

coercion theory to the consensus theory. This mistake might have been avoided by defining coercion in a more specific manner rather than using it as a blanket term. There is a sense in which even behavior issuing from a sense of moral obligation can be said to be caused by coercion. The socialized man is not an automaton; the internalization of the norms of his society does not eliminate all ambivalence from his personality. Sometimes, he is tempted to further his interest by rejecting the behavior pattern legitimized by the norms he has accepted. To behave in the socially prescribed manner in the face of such temptation, he would have to "constrain" himself from following his antisocial inclinations. We might call this internal coercion.

Consider a second meaning of coercion: A citizen is ordered by the court to pay his taxes despite his protest to the effect that his tax assessment was too high. He demurs and protests some more but pays up anyway. Clearly, he has been "forcibly" deflected from behaving in a way he would have preferred, that is, paying less tax. He may loathe the ineptitude and obstinacy of the judge and hate the tax collector without necessarily withdrawing his commitment to the institution of taxation or his loyalty to the law enforcement machinery of the state in general. Let us assume in this instance that while condemning the judge, our unhappy citizen does not question the legitimacy—I do not mean legality—of the force that the judge has exercised over him. We may call this example of coercion, legitimate coercion.

Let us consider yet another instance of coercion: the holdup man who "forces" his victim to hand him his wallet at gun point. In this case the victim feels that the "force" that has been applied to terminate his continued possession of his wallet is illegitimate, that the holdup man has no "right" to his wallet. What decides the compliance of the victim is simply a computation of "strengths"; the weaker prudently yields. In this case force means violence.

If coercion is taken in the third sense, that is as violence, then the coercion theory is untenable. For if the social order depends purely on the differential distribution of the capacity for violence, it is difficult to explain why the specialists of violence such as soldiers are not always masters. It would be implausible to explain the displacement of one set of rulers by another in any terms other than the superior (or potentially superior) capacity of the new set of rulers for violence. Indeed, to say that society is integrated by violence is in effect to deny the existence of society. For in the absence of regulatory norms and in view of the total dependence of the individuals' roles on the calculus of "strengths," we are left with the Hobbesian state of war.

If we understand coercion in the first sense, the controversy between consensus and coercion theorists becomes a rather uncomplicated semantic argument. If we take it in the second sense, then it is easy to see how the coercion theory can be integrated into the consensus theory. We can regard the use of coercion as one of the forms of social and political behavior—just like electoral campaigns, parliamentary debates, interest group articulation, or even dating—about which there is some normative consensus. In that case, it is not a relevant criticism of the consensus theory to demonstrate that coercion and conflict are ubiquitous. A more pertinent criticism would be to show that such coercion and conflict as exist in society do not for the most part take place within the context of regulatory norms and that the coercive institutions of society are not, by and large, regarded as legitimate by the members of the society.

It will not do to confine our analysis of the meaning of political integration to the level of theoretical abstraction. Our understanding of the concept of political integration will be deepened by giving the concept operational meaning. We shall try to specify how one can determine, at least crudely, the degree of integration of a historical political system.

Some Empirical Indicators of the Degree of Political Integration

1. *The Legitimacy Score.* One indication of the level of integration of a historical political system is what we may call its legitimacy score, that is, the extent to which the citizens of the state identify with the state as an embodiment of their interest and therefore concede that it deserves their loyalty and the authority to exercise certain powers over them. The legitimacy score of a given political system can be measured by attitude survey research methods, such as those used in the *Civic Culture* and *The Authoritarian Personality*.

2. *Extraconstitutional Behavior Score.* Another useful empirical indicator of the level of political integration is the frequency distribution of the preferences of political actors between constitutional and extraconstitutional actions. A political system in which political actors very frequently resort to extraconstitutional measures for pursuing their political goals is malintegrated. Some examples for extraconstitutional measures are the arbitrary arrest of political opponents, the assas-

sination of political opponents, the use of terrorism to overthrow a duly elected government. A high incidence of such extraconstitutional behavior indicates if not a lack of basic consensus about the ground rules of political competition, at least a lack of commitment to these rules; it indicates a preference for efficient over legitimate means for pursuing political goals.

While a high incidence of extraconstitutional behavior tells us that the political system is malintegrated, a low incidence of extraconstitutional behavior does not necessarily warrant the conclusion that the political system is highly integrated in the normative sense. It may simply mean that the coercive machinery of the political class is efficient.

3. *Political Violence Score.* This indicator should be distinguished from the one above. Resort to violence for achieving political goals is by definition an extraconstitutional form of behavior. But an extraconstitutional action need not take the form of political violence. The assumption behind the use of this indicator is that frequent resort to political violence means either that the development of a normative culture is still in an embryonic stage or that political actors' commitment to the existing normative culture is ambivalent or both. There is no need to elaborate on the point that a low incidence of political violence does not necessarily mean that the political system is highly integrated.

4. *Secessionist Demand Score.* Secessionism means an absence or withdrawal of commitment to the existing political system by members of the secessionist movement. The number of secessionist groups and the numerical strength of their following can therefore be

regarded as an indicator of the degree to which the political system is integrated.

5. *Alignment Pattern Score.* One additional way of determining empirically the level of integration of a political system is to analyze its political alignments patterns. The analysis should be directed towards ascertaining the extent to which the major groups (e.g., political parties) competing for control of the apparatus of government draw their support from a diversity of geographical areas and of ethnic, religious, and social and economic groups within the country. If this analysis reveals that by and large the major competing political organizations draw their support from a diversity of sociocultural and regional groups, the political system is likely to be highly integrated. Such a pattern of political alignments minimizes the politically divisive effects of sociocultural differences. It also indicates some consensus among disparate sociocultural groups about the desirability of certain collective goals and the necessity for some degree of concerted effort.

6. *Bureaucratic Ethos Score.* If a political system is highly integrated, there will be a tendency for its members to give their loyalty to the state and the constitutionally elected holders of its high offices in spite of their personal feelings about the holders of these offices. What we have christened the bureaucratic ethos score measures the extent to which loyalty of members of the political system is focused on the office rather than on the charismatic appeal of the holder of the office. The charismatic appeal of the office holder may be helpful for inducing loyalty to the office. But such loyalty is unstable as long as the charismatic authority

from which it derives is not routinized. The bureaucratic ethos score of a given political system can be determined by attitude survey research techniques.

7. *Authority Score.* The authority of the state is a function of its legitimacy score and its effectiveness for carrying out its constitutionally prescribed duties. One essential condition for carrying out its duties is the availability of coercive resources. People may accept the claims of the state as legitimate without necessarily deferring to it. This is one important reason why coercive force is so necessary for the state. The evident incapacity of the state for carrying out its legitimate functions could quite easily lead to disrespect for its authority and subsequently to a general withdrawal of commitment to the political culture. There is some justification for regarding a high incidence of the breakdown of law and order in parts of the political system (e.g., Nigeria between 1962 and 1967) as indicative of a low level of integration.

One might add that this list of empirical indicators does not pretend to be exhaustive; it is merely illustrative. It should be stressed that there are other indicators of the level of political integration which are not uniquely political in nature. For instance, a high degree of economic interdependence (economic integration) is a disincentive to politically disintegrative behavior. The degree of economic integration can be measured by the flow of goods and services between the different regions of the country. Further, within certain limits, the level of political integration is determined by the degree of social integration (the extent of the sharedness of values, goal preferences, symbols of identity, modes of communication, such as language,

common experience, etc., among members of a society).
Professor Karl Deutsch has suggested that if we regard
cultural communities as networks of communication
channels, "we can measure 'integration' of individuals
in a people by their ability to receive and transmit information on a wide range of different topics with relatively little delay or loss of relevant detail."[6] He also
suggests that social integration can also be measured by
the criterion of "interlocking roles and expectations."
We may also measure social integration by Professor
Toscano's transaction flow analysis which is a variant
of Deutsch's cybernetic model.[7]

Political integration is not usually defined as we
have defined it here. For Ernst Haas, the concept means
"a process whereby political actors in distinct national
settings are persuaded to shift their loyalties, expectations, and political activities toward a new center, whose
institutions possess or demand jurisdiction over the pre-
existing nation-state."[8] James Coleman and Carl Rosberg
conceive political integration as the "progressive bridging of the elite-mass gap on the vertical plane in the
course of developing an integrated political process and
a participant community."[9]

The process we have defined as political integration

---

[6]Karl Deutsch, *The Nerves of Government: Models of Political Communication and Control* (New York: Free Press of Glencoe, Inc., 1963) ; p.
151. See also Deutsch, *Nationalism and Social Communication: An Inquiry
into the Foundations of Nationality* (New York: M.I.T. and John Wiley &
Sons, Inc., 1953) , pp. 70–74.

[7]James Toscano, "Transaction Flow Analysis in Metropolitan Areas:
Some Preliminary Explorations," in Philip Jacob and James Toscano (eds.) ,
The Integration of Political Communities (New York and Philadelphia:
J. B. Lippincott Co., 1964) , pp. 98–119.

[8]Ernst B. Haas, *The Uniting of Europe: Political, Social and Economic Forces* (Stanford, Calif.: Stanford University Press, 1958) , p. 16.

[9]James Coleman and Carl Rosberg, *Political Parties and National Integration in Tropical Africa* (Berkeley and Los Angeles: University of California Press, 1964) , p. 9.

bears a close resemblance to the process often referred to as national integration. For instance, Leonard Binder conceptualizes the process of creating intrastate consensus, especially the bridging of the elite-mass gap, as national integration.[10] In *Nation-Building,* Karl Deutsch uses national integration in a roughly similar sense.[11] For James Coleman and Carl Rosberg, national integration subsumes two auxiliary processes: political integration, which refers to the progressive bridging of the elite-mass gap; and territorial integration, which refers to the "progressive reduction of cultural and regional tensions and discontinuities—in the process of creating a homogenous territorial political community."[12] It is clear that national integration deals with a process very similar to the one that we have described as political integration.

I have refrained from using the term national integration because "nation" suggests a highly integrated human group in the normative sense. Admittedly the concept of nation is a problematic one. But this does not affect the point. The controversy surrounding the word nation springs from the fact that different writers have explained the bond of nationality by different things—language, culture will, social communication, common history, etc. Fichte and Herder identify the essence of nationality as language,[13] Hans Kohn[14] and

---

[10]Leonard Binder, "National Integration and Political Development," *American Political Science Review,* Vol. LVII, No. 3 (September, 1964), pp. 622–63.

[11]Karl Deutsch (ed.), *Nation-Building* (New York: Atherton Press, 1963), p. 677.

[12]Coleman and Rosberg, *op. cit.,* p. 9.

[13]See Elie Kedourie, *Nationalism* (London: Hutchinson & Co., 1961), pp. 62–67.

[14]Hans Kohn, *Nationalism: Its Meaning in History* (Princeton, N.J.: D. Van Nostrand Co., Inc., 1955), p. 19, conceives nationalism as an active corporate will.

Hertz as will,[15] Hayes as cultural foundations,[16] Deutsch as social communications.[17] But each of them regards the nation as a cohesive human community. The concept national integration is, to my mind, tautological.

It remains to outline the plan of this study. Chapter 2 describes aspects of the problem of political integration in the context of the historical experience of the new states. Serious students of the new states will find nothing new in this chapter. I have stated a rather familiar problem in great detail because this seemed to me a good way to convey a sense of its complexity. Once the complexity of the problem of political integration in the new states is grasped it becomes obvious that some of the existing prescriptive theories for solving the problem are simplistic. Chapter 3 evaluates the contribution of classical sociological theory to our understanding of the problem of political integration. This chapter helps to place in proper perspective much of what is said in the three chapters following it. Classical sociological theory decisively influenced the idiom, the conceptual apparatus, and the ethico-normative assumptions of the contemporary writings on social and political integration discussed in the study.

Chapters 4 through 6 offer a critical analysis of different theoretical approaches to the problem of political integration in the new states. The approaches discussed are (in shorthand) the charismatic legitimation theory, the elite-mass gap theory, and the uniparty theory. I hope that my rather critical tone in those chapters will not be construed as a rejection of the views expressed in

---

[15]Frederick Hertz, *Nationalism in History and Politics* (3rd ed.; London: Routledge & Kegan, 1951), p. 12.

[16]Carlton J. Hayes, *Essays in Nationalism* (New York: The Macmillan Co., 1926), p. 21.

[17]Deutsch, *Nationalism and Social Communication, op. cit.*, pp. 3–4, 71–80.

these writings. My critique is concerned less with re-
vealing the weaknesses in these writings than with ex-
tracting and concretizing their many useful theoretical
hunches.

In the final chapter, it is argued that the essential
preliminary for the development of a mature political
culture in the new states is social mobilization. Yet, involving as it does a profound transformation of the social structure, social mobilization generates tensions that
threaten the very existence of the political system, whose
integration it is supposed to enhance in the long run.
This raises the question about the political content of
social mobilization: What structural characteristics must
the political system have to successfully undertake social
mobilization in the first place? What type of political
structure is best able to withstand the disruptive short-
run effects of social mobilization? The contribution of
this study lies in its attempt to answer these questions.
The theory is advanced that the political system maximizes its capacity for undertaking social mobilization
effectively and for remaining stable despite the disruptive effects of social mobilization if it is authoritarian,
paternal, "identific," and consensual. If any of these four
characteristics are absent and to the extent that functionally compensating factors are also absent, the destabilizing effects of social mobilization are increased.
Each of these key variables is discussed, and an attempt
is made to operationalize them by resolving each of them
into a set of empirical questions. Finally the theory is
tested against the experience of historical political systems—the United States of America, the Soviet Union,
Yugoslavia, Cuba, and Nigeria.

There is no need for a methodological note. This
study developed pragmatically out of many years of skep-

tical curiosity about the growing body of writings on "political development."

Research has a dynamic all its own. Start asking questions systematically about a research problem and there is no telling what turns the quest for answers may take. This study has imposed on me the necessity of making incursions into fields I am least qualified to dabble in. I have borrowed some of the less frightful concepts of contemporary sociological theory. Since I could not brave the hazards of penetrating the "sociological imagination," it may well be that my comprehension of these concepts is rather superficial. I have poached on the reserves of the historian. I prefer to think that instead of grumbling about the nuisance value of poachers, the professional historian will be gratified by the evidence of yet another nonhistorian who does not believe that "history is bunk."

Chapter 2

The Problem of
Political Integration

Introduction

The crucial problem of the postcolonial situation is the integration of the new nation which is threatened by strong centrifugal forces. The nationalist movement, invariably a coalition of ethnic, professional, religious, and social groups, tends to disintegrate with the elimination of imperial control. At the same time, the solidarity of the political leaders suffers partly because of differences in approach to the problems of administering and developing the country which now loom large. The optimistic psychological atmosphere characteristic of revolutions raises expectations to heights that the new government cannot possibly satisfy with the meager means at its disposal. The divergence of hopes and fulfillment tends to cause frustration and alienation.

Some people seek to compensate themselves for the frustrations of colonial oppression by enjoying their newly won freedom with exuberance; sometimes there is an almost pathological hatred for all forms of social and legal control. And all these tensions and cleavages

arise in a period of rapid social change when, because
many traditional usages are being abandoned and ha-
bituation to new ones is yet uncompleted, expectations
in regard to roles and responses are temporarily confused. This is the chaotic situation faced by a new government with limited experience and yet to establish its
legitimacy. The crucial problem is how to establish and
maintain authority under such difficult conditions.

Cleavages in the Nationalist Movement

Thomas Hodgkin has noted that up to a point the
colonial situation tends to promote one-party dominance.[1] Because the ending of the status of subordina-
tion is an overriding aim, the nationalist movement is
liable to assume the form of a dominant mass party
symbolizing the aspirations of the nascent nation. The
political history of the new states abounds with examples of such parties: the Tanganyika (Tanzania) African
National Union, the Kenya African National Union, the
Convention Peoples Party of Ghana, the Parti Démocratique de Guinée, the Parti Démocratique de la Côte
d'Ivoire, the Malawi Congress Party, Sierra Leone Peoples Party, the India National Congress, the Union
Progressite Sénégalaise.[2] These parties usually strive to be

---

[1] T. Hodgkin, *African Political Parties* (Baltimore: Penguin Books, 1961), p. 22.

[2] For more on these parties, see Hodgkin, *op. cit.;* and James Coleman and Carl Rosberg, *Political Parties and National Integration in Tropical Africa* (Berkeley and Los Angeles: University of California Press, 1964).

T. Hodgkin, *Nationalism in Colonial Africa* (London: Frederick Muller, 1956), pp. 137–68.

Gabriel Almond and James Coleman (eds.), *The Politics of Develop-ing Areas* (Princeton, N.J.: Princeton University Press, 1960), pp. 286–313, 406–8, and 479–511.

all things to everyone.[3] Their leaders tend to assume that
they and their parties properly incarnate all the legitimate interests of their society.[4]

However, the unity of the national party is sometimes an illusion. For it is not a body of people with a
common approach to social problems but a coalition of
special interests, each with its own particular grievance
against the colonial regime. It may include trade unions
pressing for higher wages and the ending of racial discrimination, and intellectuals angered by their subordi-
nation to semiliterate colonial officials. In addition, the
nationalist party may include syncretistic movements re-
acting against the inroads of Christianity into the native
culture, and traditional authorities smarting from their
diminishing influence. It may also include organizations
and individuals who simply hold the colonial government responsible for all social problems—poor medical
facilities, slum dwelling, juvenile delinquency, drought,
crop failure.

When the National Council of Nigeria and the
Cameroons was launched on August 26, 1944, it included 2 trade unions, 2 political parties, 4 literary societies, 8 professional associations, 11 social clubs, and
101 tribal unions.[5] In its earlier years, Burma's Anti-
Fascist Freedom League included the All-Burma Fire

[3]David Apter, *Ghana in Transition* (New York: Atheneum Publishers,
1963), p. 322, notes how the C.P.P. satisfies many social wants far beyond
what will be expected of, for example, a British party.

Kwame Nkrumah, "What the Party Stands For," *The Party*, Vol. I,
No. 1 (1960).

[4]L. Pye in Almond and Coleman (eds.), *op. cit.*, pp. 199–220.

Sékou Touré is perhaps the leading philosopher of this type of party.
See his *La Lutte du Parti Démocratique de Guinée pour la Emancipation
Africaine* (Conakry: Imprimerie Nationale, 1959). See too, Immanuel Wallerstein, "The Political Ideology of the P.D.G.," *Présence Africaine* (English
ed.), Vol. XII (First Quarter, 1962), pp. 30–44.

[5]James Coleman, *Nigeria: Background to Nationalism* (Berkeley and
Los Angeles: University of California Press, 1958, pp. 264–65.

Brigade, the St. John's Ambulance Corps, the All-Burma Teachers Organization, among other urban associations.[6] The India National Congress accommodated Hindus, Communists, Muslims, Ghandians—people with vastly different images of Indian society. It became necessary after independence to reform the party so that it became a party composed of diverse elements united by a common program.[7]

The superficiality of the atmosphere of consensus created by the nationalist movement becomes more apparent as the prospect of political autonomy improves. As each interest group maneuvers to consolidate its influence, it becomes increasingly difficult to keep up the semblance of unity, for increase in influence for one of these groups often implies loss of influence for another. If the modernizing[8] elite is to concentrate enough power to effect the massive reorganization of society which they desire, it will mean that the traditional authorities' hope of regaining power will be frustrated. An atmosphere in which every interest group is trying to insulate itself against exploitation not only endangers the solidarity of the nationalist movement but also stimulates previously politically inarticulate interest groups to seek political influence. The net effect of all this is the proliferation of political parties and the weakening of the nationalist movement.

Sudan provides an excellent example of the tendency of the nationalist movement to disintegrate with the coming of political autonomy. As Zartman's study shows, the anticolonialist agitation in Sudan ultimately

---

[6]Pye, *op. cit.*, p. 112.

[7]M. Weiner in Almond and Coleman (eds.), *op. cit.*, p. 187.

[8]Our use of the term modernization follows that of D. Micaud, *Tunisia: The Politics of Modernization* (New York: Frederick A. Praeger, Inc., 1964), pp. ix–xi.

resulted in the factionalization of politics along old ethnic and religious lines.[9] There had been some appearance of unity in the early days of the Graduates National Congress. But during the preindependence years, especially 1948–53, there was intensive factionalism. Radicals and gradualists, northerners and southerners, Khatmiya and Ansar struggled for power. The Asiqqa party allied to the Khatmiya sect, sought Arab unity, and looked to Egypt, while the Umma party advocated the creation of a national state.[10] When independence eventually came, "there was no common coin of national unity— either ethnic, socio-economic or psychological. There was no leader of stature to serve as a national symbol; the top religious and political figures were personifications of sectarianism rather than unity."[11]

This situation was by no means peculiar to Sudan. Weiner notes the tensions within the nationalist movements in India[12] and Pakistan.[13] In Ghana ethnic particularism, politically manifested in the National Liberation Movement, the Muslim Association Party, and the Northern Peoples Party, threatened the supremacy of Nkrumah's Convention Peoples Party. The Uganda National Congress was challenged by the breakaway Uganda Congress Party expressing Ganda tribalism. By 1960 the leadership of the parent Congress had split into three factions, and opposed to all these factions was the Catholic Democratic Party.[14] Similarly in Kenya, the Kenya African National Union, mainly representative of the bigger tribes such as the Luo and the Kikuyu

---

[9]I. William Zartman, *Government and Politics in Northern Africa* (New York: Frederick A. Praeger, Inc., 1963) , pp. 126–28.

[10]*Ibid.*, p. 126.

[11]*Ibid.*, p. 128.

[12]Weiner, *op. cit.*, p. 187.

[13]*Ibid.*, pp. 196–97.

[14]Coleman in Almond and Coleman (eds.) , *op. cit.*, pp. 303–4.

tribes, was opposed by the Kenya African Democratic Union, which wanted a loose federal constitution guaranteeing minority rights. In Nigeria, ethnic groups contended so bitterly that it was necessary to appoint a special commission to recommend ways of allaying minority fears.[15]

The confrontation of special interests within the nationalist movement is not the only factor that causes the weakening of the movement and the proliferation of parties. There is also the factor of the gradually expanding franchise.[16] Self-government was often approached by a gradual widening of the franchise in order systematically to increase indigenous participation. The expanding franchise gave opportunity to the politically ambitious who could organize to build new bases of power. Some of them considered that their influence would be increased by forming new political parties instead of serving a long apprenticeship as minor functionaries of the older parties.

There is also the factor of imperial diplomacy. The colonial administration sometimes encouraged the formation of conservative parties to oppose the more radical nationalist parties. Examples of such parties are the Northern Peoples Congress in Nigeria and the Northern Peoples Party in Ghana.[17] It was hoped that such parties would weaken the nationalist movement or at least temper its radicalism.[18] Better still, if the conservative party

---

[15]*The Report of the Commission Appointed to Enquire into the Fears of Minorities and the Means of Allaying Them.* Cmnd. 505.

[16]James Coleman, "The Emergence of African Political Parties," in C. Grove Haines (ed.), *Africa Today* (Baltimore, 1955). Coleman indicates that the extension of the franchise stimulated the formation of political parties.

[17]*Ibid.,* p. 23.

[18]In the case of Ghana, the formation of a conservative party only temporarily weakened the dominant Convention Peoples Party. Nigeria is the classic example of the success of this policy; the British succeeded in transferring power to the Northern Peoples Congress.

gained power, the colonial administration would enjoy the satisfaction of transferring power to moderates.

Even when the national party is not threatened by the proliferation of parties, its effectiveness and appeal may still be difficult to maintain in the postcolonial situation. One reason for this is that the passing of the struggle deprives the party of the atmosphere of crisis which makes it easy to enlist popular enthusiasm.[19] The coming of this independence tones down politics to administration, diminishes the opportunities for the leaders to dramatize their heroism, and imposes the responsibilities of office on the political leaders. At the same time, some of the party's best talents are drained off into government posts, and the efficiency of the party suffers.[20]

Again, independence may bring popular disenchantment with the national party, partly because of its failure to fulfill the expectations of those who fought under its banner[21] and partly because it is likely to be blamed for the unpopular measures now needed for rapid social and economic development. In Tanganyika (Tanzania), the popularity of the dominant Tanganyika African National Union declined after independence. One of the reasons why Julius Nyerere temporarily resigned as prime minister was because he wanted to reorganize his party. Gallagher notes the crisis in Tunisia's ruling party after 1958 which resulted from the fact that some of its more capable leaders had to divide their energy between the government and the party.[22]

It would be a mistake to assume that the history of the nationalist movement is from the day of indepen-

---

[19]C. Gallagher in Gwendolen Carter (ed.), *African One-Party States* (Ithaca: Cornell University Press, 1962), pp. 58–59.
[20]*Ibid.*, p. 60.
[21]Coleman in Almond and Coleman (eds.), *op. cit.*, pp. 296–97.
[22]Gallagher, *op. cit.*, p. 60.

dence one of inexorable, uninterrupted disintegration.[23] In spite of the tensions we have noted, some nationalist parties like the Convention Peoples party in Ghana, the India National Congress, and the Parti Démocratique de Guinée still display considerable solidarity. There are forces in the postcolonial situation which counteract the tendency of the nationalist movement to dissolve.[24] In the first place, independence gives the leaders of the dominant party some powerful instruments for enhancing their party's solidarity. Independence gives the party influence over many offices. This offers the opportunity to strengthen the party by the use of patronage. With the colonial government out of the way, the ruling party's maneuverability is vastly increased. It can, for instance, initiate a structural reorganization of local government or redraw the electoral map in order to increase its influence.

Using these pressures, some of the nationalist movements have not only survived the centrifugal pulls we discussed earlier but also consolidated their power. The Convention Peoples party of Ghana, the Kenya African National Union, the Parti Démocratique de Guinée, and the Parti Démocratique de la Côte d'Ivoire are examples of parties which in varying degrees consolidated their influence by the use of coercion and incentives.

In addition to these pressures, the dominant party seeks to maintain its influence by stigmatizing all opposition as unnecessary.[25] It can argue that the task of

---

[23]Even ethnicity is not always malintegrative. See Immanuel Wallerstein, "Ethnicity and National Integration in West Africa," *Cahiers d'Etudes Africaines*, No. 3 (October, 1960), pp. 129–39.

[24]Coleman in Almond and Coleman (eds.), *op. cit.*, p. 297, lists some of these factors.

[25]Cf. Julius Nyerere's observations in *Spearhead* (Dar-es-Salaam, November, 1961), reproduced in Paul Sigmund (ed.), *The Ideologies of Developing Countries* (New York: Frederick A. Praeger, Inc., 1963), pp. 196–202.

economic and social reconstruction is too pressing and
national goals too obvious for time to be wasted in divisive party competition. Anyone who wishes to divide
the nation must be unpatriotic or wicked. The party
can exploit the aura of legitimacy which still hallows it
because of its prominent part in the overthrow of colonialism.

The importance of these mitigating factors will depend on the skill of party leaders and the social and
political environment in which they operate. However,
it will appear, on balance, that the disintegrative pressures on the nationalist movement far outweigh these
centripetal factors. In practically every new state the
coming of independence has meant grave tensions and
cleavages. The Congo degenerated into anarchy. Other
countries have fared somewhat better. But those that
have survived with some semblance of unity have
achieved this largely by replacing the spontaneous mass
enthusiasm of the revolution with coerced conformity.
The surface may be calm, but trouble brews below.
Whether one can call this state of affairs stable is an
open debate.

Elite Competition

It is sometimes suggested that the problem of political integration is mainly one of closing the gap between the elite and the masses.[26] This view assumes that
the elite that wins power retains its cohesiveness—an
assumption that is often quite unwarranted. The coming of independence brings many cleavages to the ruling
elite just as it does to the nationalist movement. For one

[26]Edward Shils, "Political Development in the New States," *Comparative Studies in Society and History*, Vol. II (1960), pp. 265–97, 397–411.

thing, as the political leaders make the transition from shouting anti-imperialist slogans to devising concrete programs[27] for national development, differences between them begin to come into clearer relief. Radicals and gradualists,[28] modernizers and traditionalists,[29] individualists and statists, strive for influence. The situation is further complicated by the deepening rift between the older leaders and the younger generation, because as Lucian Pye suggests, the two generations have had somewhat different political experiences.[30]

The older leaders who pioneered the nationalist struggle consider themselves entitled to unquestioned obedience. But the younger generation, less complacent, more impatient to get ahead, contends that those who liberated the nation no longer have the right to misgovern her. Within the political elite a more dynamic nucleus soon emerges to demand a "second revolution." Sometimes such groups break away to form new parties. A case in point is the revolt of Mehdi ben Barka's wing of Istiqlal against the official leadership. This led to the formation in 1959 of the Union des Forces Populaires.[31]

---

[27]The leaders of the new states appreciate that their problems are greater at this stage:

"As we have already said it is easier to destroy than to build . . . the work of construction demands a great deal of sacrifice. . . ." Momady Kaba, President of the National Confederation of Guinea Workers, in a speech to a trade union conference in Bamako, Mali, in January, 1963. *Africa Report,* Vol. VIII, No. 5 (May, 1963).

See also David Apter, "Political Democracy in the Gold Coast," in C. Stillman (ed.), *Africa in the Modern World* (Chicago: University of Chicago Press, 1955), p. 134.

[28]In Mali the radicals led by Madeira Keita, former Minister of the Interior, and Henri Corethin, who had dominated the Youth Executive, clashed with President Modibo Keita. At the 1962 Party Congress, Madeira Keita was demoted and Henri Corethin was dropped from the Bureau Politique. *Africa Report,* Vol. VIII, No. 10 (November, 1963).

[29]L. Pye in Almond and Coleman (eds.), *op. cit.,* p. 129.

[30]*Ibid.*

[31]Micaud, *op. cit.,* pp. 100–101.

Similarly, in Tunisia, a new radical left formed around the *Jeune Afrique*.[32] Among its leaders were Mohammed Masmondi, Bechir Yahamed, Mohamed ben Smail, Ahmed ben Salah, and Azzou Rebai.[33] In Nigeria the radical left clustered around Otegbeye's Nigerian Youth Congress and Chike Obi's Dynamic Party.[34] In Ghana it found articulation in *Spark*,[35] and in Senegal it was symbolized by Mamadou Dia.[36]

The solidarity of the elite is further weakened by the suspicion between the intellectuals and the professional politicians. The intellectuals had been involved in the nationalist movement, for they had been among the most unhappy victims of racial discrimination. But years of denigrating the prevailing political system had habituated the intellectuals to aversion to constituted authority. This "oppositionalism" spilled over to the postcolonial regime. This alienated the indigenous politicians who, harassed by the burdens of office, tend to regard all opposition as unreasonable. The fact that a few intellectuals held government positions did not prevent the mutual alienation of intellectuals and politicians.[37] For one thing, the intellectuals tend to be even more radical than left-wing politicians.[38] This is because the intellectuals are more preoccupied with westernization, more socially and culturally isolated from the

---

[32]Gallagher, *op. cit.*, pp. 57–58.

[33]*Ibid.*

[34]Typical of the idiom of the radicals is C. Obi, *Our Struggle: A Political Analysis of the Problems of the Negro Peoples in Their Struggle for True Freedom* (Ibadan, 1954).

[35]*Spark* is a weekly published by the Bureau of African Affairs in Accra, Ghana.

[36]Edward Shils, "The Intellecturals and the Political Development of the New States," in John Kautsky (ed.), *Political Change in Underdeveloped Countries: Nationalism and Communism* (New York: John Wiley & Sons, Inc., 1962), p. 196.

[37]*Ibid.*, p. 229.

[38]Harry Brenda in Kautsky (ed.), *op. cit.*, pp. 238–41.

masses, and apt to think that the existing system does not offer them the prestige commensurate with their merit.

In some places the preindependence era saw the shifting of power from the better born, better educated leaders, who merely demanded specific social reforms, to a new generation of leaders with greater cultural affinity to the masses.[39] Nkrumah supplanted Dr. Danquah; Senghor displaced Lamine Gueye. The older leaders did not always abdicate gracefully, and it was not unusual for them to sneer at the philistinism of their successors. Silverstein notes how in Burma the older generation of leaders outside the dominant Anti-Fascist Peoples League, such as U Kyaw Min, Dr. Maung, and Dr. Ba Maw, condemned present Burmese leaders as half-educated upstarts who had failed to prove their ability in the competitive examination of colonial days.[40] The politicians on their part represent these older leaders and the intellectuals as pitiful victims of colonial indoctrination who must be reeducated and resocialized into a better appreciation of their own culture and history.[41]

Lastly, the cohesiveness of the indigenous elite is weakened by the competition for office which comes with independence.[42] However fairly the available patronage may be distributed, some people are likely to feel that they have not been adequately compensated

---

[39]T. Hodgkin, *Nationalism in Colonial Africa* (London: Frederick Muller, 1956), p. 150, claims that in Africa this new generation of postwar leaders contributed to the decline of congress-type political organization and the rise of political parties.

[40]J. Silverstein in G. Kahin (ed.), *Government and Politics in South-East Asia* (Ithaca: Cornell University Press, 1959), p. 100.

[41]See, for instance, Sékou Touré on the cultural alienation of the African intellectual: S. Touré, *L'Action Politique du Parti Démocratique pour l'Emancipation Africaine* (Conakry, 1959), esp. p. 256.

[42]David Apter, *Ghana in Transition* (New York: Atheneum Publishers, 1963), p. 312.

for their contribution to the nationalist struggle.[43] The strains within the elite caused by the scramble for office are aggravated by ethnic competition. If political leaders do not defer to the claims of their ethnic groups, they are likely to be supplanted by opportunists willing to pander to ethnic particularism.[44]

Other Cleavages in Social Structure

Another dimension of the problem of political integration is the uneasy relationship between the leaders and the masses. In the new states, there tends to exist a communication gap between the leaders and the masses, for while the former are largely westernized, the latter are still in the grip of traditional modes of thought and action. The masses are often confused by the language of secularism and rationality in which their leaders talk, while the leaders are constantly frustrated by the masses' persistence in those attitudes of mind which are clearly detrimental to the execution of the policies that will realize the cherished "brave new world."

As we have already noted, the coming of independence exacerbates the tensions between the masses and the leaders by removing the atmosphere of crisis which makes it easier to enlist the support of the masses; it

[43]Some of those involved in the attempt to assassinate President Bourguiba in December, 1962, were former members of his Neo-Destour who felt that they had not been adequately rewarded for their contribution to the national liberation movement. *Africa Report*, Vol. VIII, No. 10 (November, 1963), p. 48.

[44]The elite of the new states seems to be unable to resist the temptation to exploit ethnicity for political purposes. In Nigeria, the major political parties have ethnic bases. The Action group grew from a Yoruba cultural organization, the Egbe Omo Oduduwa; the National Council of Nigerian Citizens draws the bulk of its support from the Ibo; the Northern Peoples Congress from the Hausa and Fulani.

diminishes the opportunity for the leaders to dramatize their heroism and thereby weakens their charismatic appeal. As long as there was the colonial government, every social evil could be blamed on it. But when political autonomy comes, it becomes somewhat more difficult to find a scapegoat.[45] If the trains do not run on time, if the marketplace is dirty, if the dispensaries run out of quinine, the responsibility is laid on the indigenous elite to the peril of its popularity.

There is also the factor of popular disenchantment with the revolution and its leaders.[46] Most of the people who supported the revolution were not motivated by a passion for abstract notions of democratic rights but by expectations of material improvement. Unfortunately, these expectations are not always fulfilled. While a handful of people may improve their lot significantly, the living conditions of most people remain basically unchanged. Many are still condemned to subsistence agriculture; educational and medical facilities cannot be revolutionized overnight. Meanwhile, taxes must be paid.

Far from satisfying expectations, self-government often calls for more work, more sacrifice.[47] Those who led the liberation conceived the overthrow of the alien government merely as an essential preliminary to other ends.[48] More important than winning nominal independence was the problem of making it real.[49]

---

[45]Sometimes new scapegoats are found, e.g., neocolonialism. But this is somewhat less tangible, less visible than the colonial regime, and consequently less effective as an integrative tool.

[46]Apter, *op. cit.*, p. 312.

[47]Kwame Nkrumah, *I Speak of Freedom* (New York: Frederick A. Praeger, Inc., 1962) , pp. 90–91.

[48]Echoes of this theme abound in the pronouncements of the leaders of the new states. See Sigmund, *op. cit.*, esp. p. 186, also pp. 232–33.

No sooner is autonomy won than a tightening of the belt is called for—more taxes, more work, compulsory savings, less consumption, more stringent restraints on behavior. With characteristic ingenuity, Julius Nyerere changed Tanzania's national slogan from "Uhuru" (freedom) to "Uhuru na Kaze" (freedom means hard work).[50] L. Gray Cowan notes how in the process of adapting French colonial law to independent Guinea, the ruling Parti Démocratique de Guinée has introduced penalties frequently more severe than those of French colonial law. For instance, theft is now punishable by death.[51]

To all this must be added the frictions and feelings of harassment generated by the massive reshaping of the attitudes of the masses to which the leaders are committed. There is first the process that Sékou Touré calls "integral decolonization."[52] This means the neutralization of colonial indoctrination, "the total reconversion of the human being who has been taught a way of thinking foreign to the real condition of his milieu."[53] More important still is the process of socializing the masses into the rational-bureaucratic culture on which the success of the drive for industrialization depends.[54]

---

[49]Cf. Patrice Lamumba, *Congo My Country* (London: Pall Mall, 1962), p. 150. "Congo's independence can only be real when it is strong enough intellectually, technically, and materially."

[50]"You remember our previous slogan was 'Self-Government Now' . . . Now it is 'Freedom.' Let the old slogan give us a new one, namely 'Serve Ghana Now.'" Nkrumah, *I Speak of Freedom, op. cit.*, p. 92.

[51]L. G. Cowan in Carter (ed.), *op. cit.*, p. 214.

[52]*Ibid.*, p. 194.

[53]*Ibid.*

[54]On the problem of adapting the traditional culture to industrialization, see A. Richards (ed.), *Economic Development and Tribal Change* (Cambridge, 1954).

Enlargement of the Exchange Economy in Tropical Africa, United Nations Department of Economic Affairs, Doc. No. E/2557St/ECA/23, March, 1954.

People have to be persuaded (or forced) to send their children to school, to put their money in savings banks rather than burying it in the ground, to avail themselves of the advantages of insecticides and irrigation.

The Problems of Policy

This picture of the cleavages of the new states suggests by its complexity that some of our current prescriptions for integrating these societies are simplistic. Indeed, the problem of integrating the new state is so complex that an attempt to tackle one aspect of it is likely to aggravate another. Wriggins illustrates this problem in his study of Ceylon. If Ceylonese leaders desire to identify with their people, they must attempt to elicit their support. But, insofar as most people are still moved only by appeals to traditional ties, they are obliged to indulge to some extent the masses' ethnic particularism. But to make this concession is to impede progress toward broader state identity.[55]

Again, it will be desirable for the new state to officially adopt one of the indigenous languages. Such a step will help to reduce cultural fragmentation while enhancing the country's identity. Unfortunately, such reform can precipitate serious dissension. In Ceylon the Tamils bitterly opposed the effort of the Sinhalese majority to raise the status of Sinhalese.[56] The attempt to make Hindi the official language raised a political storm in India. In Nigeria there has been talk about making Hausa the official language, but nothing has been done

---

[55]W. H. Wriggins, "Impediments to Unity in the New States: The Case of Ceylon," *American Political Science Review,* Vol. LV, No. 2 (June, 1961), p. 314.

[56]*Ibid.*

in this direction because of the fear of the sharp reaction that is anticipated from the Yorubas and Ibos.

Similar difficulties beset educational reform. In Ceylon, an attempt to teach the higher grades in vernacular resulted in more children leaving school without the unifying experience of learning English. The vernacular press grew with literacy and intensified ethnic competition between Sinhalese and Tamils.[57]

Nor is it easier to find cultural symbols around which the country may be united. Wriggins points out that when Ceylon cast round for a cultural symbol from her past, it was discovered that the past had no common significance for all Ceylonese.[58] Ceylonese recalled battles won and lost from each other. What some remembered as the hour of heroism was remembered by others as the hour of humiliation. It was clear that the quest for a symbol of identity from the Ceylonese past could only underline the inferiority and superiority feelings among the various ethnic groups to the detriment of integration.

Marriot notes similar difficulties in regard to the Mogul symbolism in the Indian government.[59] The adoption of this symbolism was, of course, inevitable since India's capital city and much of its present institutional apparatus are imbued with the Mogul past. However, India's rulers have to be cautious with Mogul identification. Pressed too far, this symbolism could alienate the Muslims, who consider Akbar a heretic, and the Hindus and Sikhs, who recall Moguls as bloody conquerors.[60] Marriot notes that the choice of the Buddhist

---

[57]*Ibid.,* p. 316.

[58]*Ibid.*

[59]M. Marriot, "Cultural Policy in the New States," in Clifford Geertz (ed.), *Old Societies and New States: The Quest for Modernity in Asia and Africa* (New York: Free Press of Glencoe, Inc., 1963), p. 34.

[60]*Ibid.*

Emperor Asoka as the patron saint of the nation was not due to the fact that he was more exciting than the legendary dynasties of the Mahabharata, but was simply that he belonged to no known caste, no embattled region, and was a native ruler with spiritual pretensions.[61]

Conclusion

We have stated this familiar problem in rather tiresome detail in order to underline its complexity. As will become increasingly clear, our description of the problem of political integration is an important aspect of our general critique. A major defect of current theories of political integration is their insensitiveness to the complexity of the problem with which they are concerned. Because they oversimplify the question, they are prone to offer superficial answers. It is clear, for instance, that those theories which conceive political integration mainly as the bridging of the sociocultural gap between the elite and the masses are inadequate. For, as this chapter shows, the elite-mass dichotomy is only one—and by no means the most important—dimension of the problem.

It must be frankly admitted that the complexity of our problem has not been fully portrayed in this chapter. Some factors, such as tribalism, could bear more rigorous exploration; others like racism (in the multiracial states) have been left out in order to keep our exposition within manageable scope.[62] Perhaps we should have balanced to a greater degree the pessimistic picture

---

[61]*Ibid.*, p. 35.

[62]J. Coleman, "The Problem of Political Integration in Emergent Africa," *Western Political Quarterly*, Vol. VIII, No. 1 (March, 1955), pp. 44–58.

we have drawn. We could have emphasized the unifying potential of Christianity[63] and Islam,[64] the language and the political philosophy of the metropolitan countries, the bonds of wider economic interaction, the fact that the disintegration of some traditional ties is an essential preliminary to the forging of wider bonds. But then this would again bring new complications. For example, as the experience of Nigeria, Niger Republic, Sudan, and Uganda shows, neither Islam nor Christianity is an unmitigated blessing to political integration.

[63]G. Carpenter, "The Role of Christianity and Islam in Contemporary Africa," in Haines (ed.) , *op. cit.*

[64]Alphonse Gouilly, *L'Islam dans L'Afrique Occidentale Francaise* (Paris: Larousse, 1952) .

Chapter 3

Political Integration
and Social Theory

This chapter outlines and evaluates the contributions of classical social theory to our understanding of the problem of political integration. The writings of Marx, Weber, Spencer, Simmel, Maine, St. Simon, Toennies, Comte, and Durkheim are particularly relevant to the purposes of this study. Their relevance lies in the fact that they have decisively influenced the idiom, conceptual apparatus, and ethico-normative assumptions of contemporary writings on political integration. More than that, they provide insights that facilitate the development of a theory of political integration.

Karl Marx's contribution to our understanding of the process of political integration arises from his attempt to grapple with alienation, the perennial problem of German philosophy which had been posed in a singularly provocative form by Hegel. Hegel had postulated that man is God (the Absolute Spirit) in his self-alienation, and that history is the development of the

Spirit in time, that is, the process by which the Spirit regains its self-identity.[1]

Revolting against Hegel, Feuerbach had insisted that Hegelianism was "rational mysticism," the last grandiose prop of decadent Christianity.[2] In his *Essence of Christianity*, Feuerbach reverses the position of Hegel. God, Feuerbach argues, is man in his self-alienation. Man is the real God for since the self-consciousness of God first arises in the consciousness which man has of God, the human consciousness is the divine consciousness.[3] There are not two worlds—only one, the material world—and God is merely the projection of man's imagination caused by his self-estrangement.

Marx agreed with Feuerbach that the material world is the only real world, but he emphasized that this world is a field of alienation.[4] Feuerbach, he insisted, had left uncompleted the task of liberating man. Thanks to Feuerbach, the religious world had been dissolved into its secular basis. But the main task remains to be done: the secular world must be revolutionized by removing its contradictions.[5]

Marx found that alienation was inherent in capitalist society. The captalist mode of production implies the concentration of the means of production in the hands of a few persons;[6] it implies the capitalist's "un-

---

[1]Hegel, *Philosophy of History* (New York: Dover Publications, 1956), p. 72.

[2]R. Tucker, *Philosophy and Myth in Karl Marx* (New York: Columbia University Press, 1961), p. 72.

[3]L. Feuerbach, *The Essence of Christianity* (New York: Harper & Bros., 1957), p. 83.

[4]Karl Marx, "Thesen über Feuerbach," *Karl Marx und Friedrich Engels, Werke*, Institut fur Marxismus-Leninismus Beim Zk Sed (Dietz Verlag Berlin, 1959), Band 3, pp. 533–34.

[5]*Ibid.*, p. 534.

[6]Karl Marx, *Capital: A Critical Analysis of Capitalist Production*, trans. S. Moore and E. Aveling (Moscow: Foreign Language Publishing House, 1961), Vol. I, p. 355.

disputed authority over men that are but parts of a mechanism that belong to him."[7] Above all, it implies the life-long annexation of the laborer to a monotonous, psychologically unsatisfying, partial operation.[8] In the capitalist society, anarchy reigns in the social division of labor, despotism in the workshop, and each of these conditions reinforces the other.[9] The effect of this type of social organization is the alienation of the masses, for in capitalist society, the worker has neither a sense of dignity nor a feeling of identity with the larger social whole. Since alienation is inherent in capitalist society, the only way to cure it is the total abolition of capitalist society.[10]

Marx's works do not constitute a theory of political integration but a philosophy of history. He tries to demonstrate at great length the movement of history toward the socialist paradise, rather than giving us a detailed picture of the new society. The insight he provides on political integration lies in the way he shows that certain forms of economic relations lead to alienation, that if the individual is to identify with his society, if social tension is to be minimal, society must be seen to be the condition for the satisfaction of the material and emotional needs of its members.

Like Marx, Weber was a product of the German historical school.[11] Like Marx, he was concerned with the systematization of detailed historical studies of vari-

---

[7]*Ibid.*, p. 356.

[8]Karl Marx and Frederick Engels, *The Communist Manifesto,* authorized English translation. Edited and annotated by Frederick Engels (New York: New York Labor News Co., 1964) , pp. 22–23.

[9]Marx, *Capital,* Vol. I., *op. cit.,* p. 356.

[10]Marx and Engels, *The Communist Manifesto,* pp. 32–33, 58, 65–67.

[11]T. Parsons, *The Structure of Social Action* (London and New York: McGraw-Hill Book Co., Inc., 1937) , p. 502.

ous epochs. Both men characterized the socioeconomic system of the modern West as "rational bourgeois capitalism."[12] But, while Marx identified the central feature of rational bourgeois capitalism as the class struggle, Weber identified it as the rational organization of labor, which was, in turn, a feature of a more general type of social organization—bureaucracy. Bureaucracy is the "fitting of individuals' actions into a complicated pattern in such a way that the character of each and its relations to the rest can be accurately controlled in the interest of the end to which the whole is devoted."[13] Empirically associated with this form of social organization is a set of values, the *geist* of capitalism nourished by the Protestant ethic.[14] Weber saw social evolution as a movement from traditionalistic social systems, whose legitimacy is based on custom, to bureaucratic systems.[15]

As in the case of Marx, what emerges from an analysis of Weber's writings is a theory of social evolution. His description of his bureaucratic and traditionalistic types, which represent in effect different types of integration, and his analysis of the consequences of these forms of integration illuminate the phenomenon of political integration. Weber teaches that the more a system of authority legitimized by rational-legal values exhibits bureaucratic structural features, the more effective it is; that is, the greater the compliance with the directives issued.

---

[12]*Ibid.*, p. 505.

[13]*Ibid.*, p. 507.

[14]This idea is developed in Max Weber, *The Protestant Ethic and the Spirit of Capitalism*, trans. T. Parsons (New York: Charles Scribner's Sons, 1958) , esp. pp. 155–83.

[15]Max Weber, *The Theory of Social and Economic Organization*, trans. T. Parsons and A. M. Henderson (New York: Free Press of Glencoe, Inc., 1964) , p. 341.

Marx and Weber were not alone in postulating the tendency of societies to pass from one form of structure to another. This notion is also present in the works of Henry Maine and Ferdinand Toennies. In *Ancient Law,* Maine points out that the movement of progressive societies has been uniform in one respect: the tendency for contract to replace status as the basis of association. "Starting as from one terminus of history, from a condition of society in which all the relations of persons are summed up in relations of family, we seem to have steadily moved toward a phase of social order in which all these relations arise from the free agreement of individuals."[16] While family dependency dissolved, individual obligation grew; the individual gradually replaced the family as the unit of social organization.[17]

Maine's analytic categories, status and contract, correspond to Toennies' *Gemeinschaft* and *Gesellschaft.* Toennies considered that there was a universal movement from a social order based on consensus of wills and nourished by mores and religion to a social order based on convention and agreement. The former is characterized by natural will *(Wesenwille),* and the latter by rational will *(Kurwille).* In its most elementary form, "natural will means nothing more than a direct, naive, and therefore emotional volition."[18] Rational will is most frequently characterized by consciousness, especially the calculation of ends and means. Toennies calls "all kinds of associations in which natural will predominates, *Gemeinschaft,*" and all those which are formed

---

[16]Henry Maine, *Ancient Law: Its Connection with the Early History of Society and Its Relation to Modern Ideas* (Boston: Beacon Press, 1963), pp. 168, 261.

[17]*Ibid.*

[18]Ferdinand Toennies, "Gemeinschaft and Gesellschaft," trans. C. P. Loomis, *Fundamental Concepts of Sociology* (New York: American Book Co., 1940), p. 17.

and "fundamentally conditioned by rational will, *Gesell-schaft.*"[19]

Again, in Toennies we find no articulated theory of social and political integration. The relevance of his work to the problem of integration lies in his identification of various forms of integration. This underlines the point already made that integration is not an undifferentiated phenomenon. Toennies himself would not have claimed more. As he pointed out, his ideal types, *Gemeinschaft* and *Gesellschaft,* are concepts signifying "the modal qualities of essence and the tendencies of being bound together."[20]

Our examination of the contribution of classical sociology to the illumination of the problem of political integration would not be complete without mentioning Simmel, St. Simon, Comte, Spencer, and Durkheim. The contributions of these scholars are of essentially the same nature as those of Marx, Toennies, Weber, and Maine. They offer no maximizing theories of political integration; at best, they offer descriptions of various forms of integration and an explanation of the conditions which sustain them. What distinguishes this group from the people that we have already discussed is their belief that the modern form of integration which has come with industrialization promises greater stability and better opportunities for increasing individual and social welfare than the older forms.

Marx believed in the superiority of the socialist paradise, but he was more interested in demonstrating the inexorable movement of history toward it than in giving a clear picture of its structure. Weber acknowledged that bureaucratic organization was superior to

---

[19]*Ibid.*
[20]*Ibid.*, pp. 17–18.

any other in stability, precision, and reliability.[21] But he was afraid that bureaucratization would lead to "bureaucratic absolutism."[22] He despaired at the thought of a world of "those little cogs, little men clinging to little jobs and striving toward higher ones."[23]

Maine and Toennies were more interested in showing trends than in indicating their preferences. Toennies was somewhat pessimistic about *Gesellschaft*-like society. In his later work, *Geist der Neuzeit,* he looks back with nostalgia to the *Gemeinschaft*-like Middle Ages, contrasting its unity and "solicitous paternalism" with the atomization and compulsory exploitation of his time.[24] With Simmel, St. Simon, Comte, and Durkheim, we come to a rather more enthusiastic acceptance of the emerging industrial society and a more sustained effort to demonstrate its superiority to previous social structures in efficiency and solidarity.

Like most classical sociologists, Simmel had a theory of social development. He thought that the basis of group affiliation was becoming increasingly "rational," rather than "mechanical." According to Simmel, the individual was, in previous times, implicated in a web of circumstances that imposed on him a close coexistence with those whom the accident of birth placed next to him.[25] At this stage, he is said to belong to a primary group. As society develops, the individual establishes for himself contacts with persons outside the primary

21Weber, *The Theory of Social and Economic Organization, op. cit.,* p. 337.

22R. Bendix, *Max Weber: An Intellectual Portrait* (New York: Doubleday & Co., 1960) , pp. 445–46.

23*Ibid., p.* 455.

24Loomis, *op. cit.,* p. ix.

25George Simmel, *Conflict: The Web of Group Affiliation,* trans. K. Wolff and R. Bendix (New York: Free Press, 1964) , pp. 127–28.

group but related to him in regard to "inclinations, activities, and talents." Thus, secondary groups develop.

In general, Simmel argues, this new type of group affiliation enlarges the sphere of freedom because it makes affiliation a matter of choice.[26] In order to build a stable organization, it is expedient to organize affiliation around intellectually articulated interests.[27] Primary groups become really effective only through "mediation, reflection, and conscious striving."[28] Simmel saw that once the individual begins to choose his associates according to his interests, skills, and personality, he involves himself in a multiplicity of groups, and that this raises problems. The security which goes with being a member of a primary group gives way to uncertainty; the individual may become a victim of psychological tensions, or even a "schizophrenic break."[29]

Simmel was, however, more impressed by the advantages of multigroup affiliation. He argues that multigroup affiliation strengthens the coordination of the individual's personality. According to Simmel, conflicting and integrating tendencies are mutually reinforcing, for conflicting tendencies arise precisely because the individual has a core of inner unity.[30] The more the ego becomes conscious of this inner unity the more it is confronted with the task of reconciling with itself a diversity of group interests.[31] This theory of social evolution is not significantly different from those we have already outlined and it is unnecessary for us to repeat

---

[26]*Ibid.*, p. 130.
[27]*Ibid.*
[28]*Ibid.*, p. 134.
[29]*Ibid.*, p. 141.
[30]*Ibid.*, p. 142.
[31]*Ibid.*

the points we have already made as to the limitations of seeking illumination on political integration from such theories.

For St. Simon,[32] the social evolution of European societies falls into three successive stages: the theological or feudal, the metaphysical or juridical, and the positive or industrial. Each of these categories was at once an ontological perspective and a form of social organization.[33] In *L'Industrie*, St. Simon argues that European civilization had reached a state in which the only normal form that collective activity could henceforth take was industrial.[34] The old religious and military virtues had, according to St. Simon, lost their relevance. The only interest now capable of supplying the nucleus of social life is economic interest:

Il est un ordre d'intérêts senti par tous les hommes, les intérêts qui appartiennent à l'entretien de la vie et au bien-être. Cet ordre d'intérêts est le seul sur lequel tous les hommes s'entendent et aient besoin de s'accorder, le seul où ils aient à délibérer, à agir en commun. . . .[35]

The analytic categories of St. Simon were later to echo in Comte's famous law of three stages. Both Comte and St. Simon were directly concerned not with integration but with establishing the law of progress. Their contribution to political integration is limited to the occasional flashes of insight which we get from their analysis of the three successive social orders, which represent different forms of integration, and their case

---

[32]For an excellent analysis of St. Simon's social theories, see Emile Durkheim, *Socialism*, trans. C. Sattler (Yellow Springs, Ohio: Antioch Press, 1962).

[33]This view is argued in his *L'Organisateur* (1819). See E. Dentu (ed.), *Oeuvres de Saint-Simon et D'Enfantin* (Paris: Libraire de la Société des Gens de Lettre, 1869), Vol. IV.

[34]St. Simon, *L'Industrie*, in Dentu (ed.), *op. cit.*, Vol. II, pp. 186–88.

[35]*Ibid.*, p. 188.

for the more solidary nature of the emerging industrial society.

Herbert Spencer's interest in integration was more direct. He saw a parallel between social and biological evolution. In Spencer's view, social evolution derives its dynamic from the continuous interplay of the forces of integration and differentiation. First, under the influence of external stimuli, especially war, the social organism undergoes an increase in integration. This gives rise to a "dissipation of motion," which causes greater functional differentiation in the social structure.

Spencer distinguished between two types of societies, the "military" and the "industrial," each characterized by a different principle of integration. The principle of integration in the military type of society is "compulsory cooperation." The military chief wields political authority, and the individual is subordinated to this authority.[36] The principle of integration in the industrial society is voluntary cooperation. In this type of society, the individual is freed from the tyranny of the state and allowed to enter freely chosen contractual relationships. In effect, the principle of integration in industrial society is the principle of freedom. Statism is avoided in the interest of individual spontaneity; society is held together by the web of relationships into which individuals have entered in their mutual interest.

This, again, is a theory of social evolution. But, unlike most of the writers we have treated, Spencer does more than identify various forms of integration. He explores in some detail not only the principles underlying these forms of integration but also their general conse-

---

[36]Herbert Spencer, *Principles of Sociology* (London: Williams & Norgate, 1897), Vol. III, esp. p. 484.

quences. But Spencer's contribution to our understanding of political integration is somewhat limited by the
nature of his theory. If we may assume that the maintenance of a stable social order demands the blending
of coercion and spontaneous conformity, the analytic
usefulness of Spencer's typologies—compulsory and voluntary—is questionable. For it is misleading to dichoto-
mize these complementary aspects of social unity. Again,
Spencer's theory smacks of the fallacy of the invisible
hand. Can we minimize the discontinuities likely to beset a system depending purely on voluntary individual
exchanges?

With Emile Durkheim we come to still more direct
concern with integration. His *The Division of Labor in
Society* was inspired by the problem of the relation of
the individual to social solidarity. Durkheim had observed what seemed to him a paradoxical phenomenon:
the individual while becoming more autonomous was
depending more on society.[37] He found the explanation
in the transformation of society—essentially the "efface-
ment" of segmental structures—which had led to a progressive development of the division of labor. As a
result of this transformation, a special order based on
mechanical solidarity and characterized by penal law
was being gradually supplanted by a new social order
based on organic solidarity and characterized by resti-
tutive law.

Mechanical solidarity is a feature of lower societies.
Such societies draw their life from the "common conscience," which is "the totality of beliefs and sentiments
common to the average citizen" and which determines
his social behavior.[38] These collective values penetrate

---

[37]Emile Durkheim, *The Division of Labor in Society,* trans. George
Simpson (New York: The Macmillan Co., 1933), p. 37.
[38]*Ibid.,* p. 79.

the individual completely. Everyone recognizes his sta-
tion and its duties. Everyone recognizes when a crime
has been committed, and reaction to the crime is "spontaneous, concerted, and unopposed."[39]

In the case of organic solidarity, the focus of interest shifts from the collective conscience to the individual. The collective conscience is, as it were, plural-
ized. The individual becomes differentiated by the
social function that he performs. He is no longer forced
into a rigid mode of living determined by his heredity
but orders his life according to his abilities, inclinations,
and opportunities.[40]

Durkheim argues that organic solidarity is morally
superior and more lasting than mechanical solidarity.
Lower societies break down easily.[41] The Kalmucks and
Mongols abandon their chief when they find him too
oppressive; the Abipones could leave their chief without as much as incurring his displeasure; the Balondas
and the Koukis emigrate incessantly.[42] Durkheim observes that it is paradoxical that a tie (mechanical solidarity) which binds the individual to the community
by absorbing him so completely into it can be made
and broken so easily. He explains this by pointing out
that it is one thing for a social tie to be rigid and another for it to have resistive force. Mechanical solidarity
lacks resistive force because it is not a totality of mutually complementary parts. Since the parts of the social
body do not really need each other, as each contains
within itself the social life, the part can sever itself from
the whole without great discomfort.

It is otherwise with organic solidarity. Because the

39*Ibid.*, pp. 74–75.
40*Ibid.*, p. 182.
41*Ibid.*, p. 148.
42*Ibid.*, p. 149.

different parts of the social whole perform different functions, each of which has some significance for the general well-being, the part cannot with convenience break away. He cites Spencer's remark to the effect that if we separate Middlesex from its surrounding district, its economic activities will grind to a halt in a few days.[43] Durkheim argues that the division of labor reinforces the feeling of solidarity between two or more persons. Precisely because man and woman are different, they seek each other.[44] However, reciprocity of feeling is not brought about by contrast per se. Only those differences which are mutually complementary nourish reciprocal feelings. However endowed we may be, we always lack something. Therefore, we seek in our friends the qualities that we lack, and in associating with them, we participate to some degree in their nature and thus feel less incomplete.[45]

These are valuable insights into integration. But Durkheim's view is not without its problems. Theoretically it is conceivable that the division of labor may heighten the individual's feeling of insufficiency by isolating him in some obscure, monotonous operation. A complex division of labor may reduce the individual to an insignificant cog in a vast machine, and this may lead to alienation. Durkheim himself recognized this fact. He tried to deal with it in the preface to the second edition of his *The Division of Labor in Society*. Durkheim was aware that the division of labor in a setting such as the factory does not have some of the integrative effects of the "division of labor in society."

---

[43]Spencer, *op. cit.*, Vol. III, p. 381.
[44]Durkheim, *The Division of Labor in Society, op. cit.*, p. 56.
[45]*Ibid.*, pp. 55–56.

Conclusion

This brief survey reveals how the analytic categories of classical social theory have become indispensable
for analyzing social change in the developing countries.
It is now common practice to characterize the original
social order of these countries as traditional (following
Weber) and the end product of their evolution as an
individualistic or a rational-bureaucratic social order.

We often explain the social and psychological tensions of these transitional societies in terms of dissolu-
tion of the older social ties of blood and lineage and
the yet uncompleted development of bonds based on
personality, skill, and interest. Implicitly, we conceive
the social development of the emerging nations in the
idiom of Maine's status and contract, Toennies' *Gemeinschaft* and *Gesellschaft*, Weber's traditional and bureaucratic orders, and Durkheim's mechanical and organic
solidarity.

Beyond giving us a ready tool for analyzing different social structures, classical social theory gives us useful information on the modes and conditions of integration. For instance, from Marx we learn how the
economic structure of society determines its solidarity.
Weber's analysis indicates that the regularizing of expectations is an important prerequisite of integration.
Durkheim reminds us that if a society is to be integrated and have resistive force, its component parts must
be functionally complementary.

The writings we have examined describe the conditions of social solidarity, but they do not give us a detailed picture of the genesis of these conditions; they
describe broad evolutionary trends, but they do not give

us a clear picture of how men's day-to-day decisions and actions galvanize the forces that determine these evolutionary trends. Even for Marx, human action was relatively (i.e., to the mystical forces of history) unimportant.

The task of nation-building in the new states may be approached as one of creating the conditions of social and political solidarity laid down in these sociological writings. For instance, in terms of Weber's terminology, nation-building in the new states may be seen as a matter of reducing an aggregation of traditional societies to a single rational bureaucratic structure.

When we approach the conditions of social solidarity found in classical sociological theory as products of social engineering rather than of slow social evolution, the complexity of the problem of nation-building comes into clearer relief. For we then begin to confront many new and difficult questions. What are the requisite social, economic, and political policies for creating these conditions? What socioeconomic and political structure is most conducive to the successful implementation of these policies? Are those policies likely to generate grave tensions? If so, how are these tensions to be "managed"?

Chapter 4

Charismatic Legitimation

and

Political Integration

This chapter examines an approach to the problem of political integration which we may categorize as
the theory of charismatic legitimation. The theory of
charismatic legitimation addresses itself to the question
as to how the state comes to be the primary focus of
the individual's loyalties when to begin with these loyalties were formerly focused on parochial institutions
such as the chieftaincy or the tribal council. The theory
suggests that one mechanism by which such transfer of
loyalties may come about is the charismatic leader whose
appeal to a number of people differing considerably in
many respects (e.g., tribe, class) can be manipulated to
transfer political loyalties from parochial to ecumenical
levels.

Before going into a discussion of charismatic legitimation, it must be pointed out that none of the authors
we shall be discussing, namely Weber, Wallerstein, Apter, Runciman, and Horowitz, uses charisma as the ful-

crum of a general theory to explain integration or the lack of it. "The theory of charismatic legitimation" is merely a shorthand term for describing their treatment of charisma as an important transitional phenomenon which can further political integration. It is hoped that a systematic discussion of what seems to us a common element in the thought of these authors can be carried on without giving the misleading impression that they constitute a body of thought.

Wallerstein's phrasing of the problem of political integration in the new state is that the government does not command "the residual loyalty" of most of its citizens.[1] In the final analysis, Wallerstein argues, integration can only be presumed to have taken place when the citizen accepts the state "as the legitimate holder of force and authority, the rightful locus of legislation and social decision."[2] The legitimation of the state is a matter of getting the citizen to regard it as a genuine representative of his interests and, therefore, deserving his loyalty; it is to some extent a matter of making him think of the state as "we" rather than "they."[3]

For Wallerstein the main instruments for legitimating the new state are the dominant political party[4] and the charismatic leader. He conceptualizes the functions of the party in the following way: it communicates ideas between the government and the people; its cadres educate the citizenry and enlist support for government policies; it strengthens social solidarity with its ideology and enables integration to be accomplished in a manner

---

[1]Immanuel Wallerstein, *Africa: The Politics of Independence* (New York: Vintage Books, 1961), p. 87.

[2]*Ibid.*, p. 88.

[3]*Ibid.*, p. 91.

[4]He is referring mainly to the one-party states, e.g., Ivory Coast, Mali, Ghana, Tanzania, Kenya.

which maximizes mass participation.[5] Nevertheless, the party is only the structure by which the unifying influence of the charismatic leader assumes a stable and tangible mold.

In the context of the new state, political integration involves changing the focus of group loyalty from a traditional to a bureaucratic structure; that is, supplanting a corporate unity based on loyalty to an authority legitimized by tradition with a corporate unity based on the acceptance of rationally chosen rules.[6] For the most part, the citizens of the new states are still in the grip of their traditional institutions and are unlikely to accept without hesitation the claims of the state to their loyalty.

The theory of charismatic legitimation posits that the recognition of the authority of the state is facilitated if the state's claims are put forward by someone whom the masses respect and trust. In other words, the theory assumes that the masses respect the charismatic leader in a way they do not respect the state and that this personal respect can be used to buttress the state until it wins its own legitimacy. "The charismatic justification for authority ('do it because I, your leader, say so') can be seen as a way of transition, an interim measure which gets people to observe the requirements of the nation out of loyalty to the leader while they . . . learn to do so for its own sake."[7]

Wallerstein recognizes that the charismatic leader may fail to legitimate the state. Like other human beings, the leader is prone to make mistakes and antagonize people.[8] He sometimes has a bad press at home

---

[5]*Ibid.*, pp. 96–99.
[6]*Ibid.*, p. 99.
[7]*Ibid.*
[8]*Ibid.*, pp. 100–101.

and abroad. His appeal may be weakened by intellectuals who oppose the mass hysteria and the cults of irrationality and personality allegedly associated with charismatic politics. Because of these factors, the masses may become disenchanted with the charismatic leader. Consequently, he may not command sufficient prestige to legitimate the state. But Wallerstein indicates that the erosion of charisma can be checked by flamboyant ceremonies, ceaseless glorification, and occasional religious sanctification of the leader.[9]

A similar theory of integration is to be found in David Apter's *Ghana in Transition*. The theme of this work is political institutional transfer—"the kind of adaptation and adjustment which those hitherto tribal peoples of the Gold Coast (Ghana) have made in order to operate parliamentary democracy on a national scale."[10] Unlike some specialists on African studies, Apter has the penetration to see the elements of the traditional social structures which facilitate the shift in orientation to the secular state. He finds that the Ashanti Confederation was characterized by a clear distinction between the individual and his office, limited functions of authority, and a hierarchic administrative structure.[11] Since these elements of social structure are compatible with bureaucratic society, the process of political institutional transfer need not exterminate every vestige of traditional society.

Nevertheless, he does not overlook the fact that political institutional transfer is fundamentally disruptive of indigenous society. For political institutional transfer to take place, many institutions and usages that

[9]*Ibid.*

[10]David Apter, *Ghana in Transition* (New York: Atheneum Publishers, 1963), p. 8.

[11]*Ibid.*, p. 291.

were critically important for maintaining the indigenous sociocultural system have to be substantially modified or abandoned.[12] In such circumstances, the collapse of the social system can only be avoided by introducing a new social structure to serve as a nucleus of unity.[13] The charismatic leader, Nkrumah, was the nucleus.

Through the charisma of Nkrumah, Ghanaians of diverse tribal origins found a close and intimate solidarity. In a society changing so rapidly that the individual's sense of direction was imperiled by uncertainty, Nkrumah provided psychological comfort.[14] He held together those whom the slackening bonds of tradition had left with no common identity; he emboldened those wishing to escape the nagging constraints of tradition.[15] Faith in Nkrumah's wisdom sustained those whose evaluative criteria had been thrown into confusion by rapid social change.

How was Nkrumah able to fulfill this role? What was the effective source of his charisma? Nkrumah's charismatic appeal came from his functional identity with the chieftaincy. He appropriated the chief's authority by meeting the same functional requirements, albeit through new social structures.[16] The chief was, at the same time, "a symbolic referrent," an "integrational integer," a "sanctional source," and the criterion of ethnic definition.[17] Nkrumah fulfilled all those functions. He became the source of new norms, and it was in accordance with these norms that his followers were to organize their behavior.

12*Ibid.*
13*Ibid.*, p. 274.
14*Ibid.*, p. 304.
15*Ibid.*
16*Ibid.*
17*Ibid.*, pp. 304–5.

Both Wallerstein and Apter see charismatic authority as a halfway house, mediating between the traditional
societies and the modern bureaucratic state. In Apter's
words, "as charisma has worked . . . as a newly accepted
source of legitimacy, it has provided for the public extension of legitimacy and support to new types of social
structures in keeping with the objectives of nationalism meanwhile retaining sub-relational aspects of the
traditional system, and integrating these aspects in different relational and behavioral modes permissible by
Nkrumah's sanction."[18]

It is important to make a few points about the concept of charisma before going into an evaluation of this
theory. Max Weber's concept of charisma has been criti-
cized on several grounds.[19] For instance, Carl Friedrich
has suggested that charisma does not provide an adequate type of leadership but only of power.[20] Power is
differentiated according to its source, leadership according to its functions.[21] Leadership presupposes the existence of structured power, that is, institutionalized
power. But, since charisma is the very antithesis of structured power, it is not clear what charismatic leadership
means.

Dorothy Emmet suggests that Weber has concep-
tualized charisma too narrowly and assimilated it too

[18]*Ibid.*, p. 303.

[19]For a general critique of Weber's typologies of authority, see P. Blau
and W. Scott, *Formal Orgnization: A Comparative Approach* (San Francisco:
Chandler Publishing Co., 1963) , pp. 30–36; Peter Blau, "Critical Remarks on
Weber's Theory of Authority," *American Political Science Review*, Vol. LVII
(1963) , pp. 305–16; Carl Friedrich *et al., Nomos*, Vol. I, pp. 28 ff.; Carl Friedrich, *Zeitschrift fur Politik*, Vol. VII (1960) , pp. 1 ff.

[20]Carl Friedrich, "Political Leadership and the Problem of Charismatic
Power," *Journal of Politics*, Vol. XXIII, No. 1 (February, 1961) , pp. 3–24.

[21]*Ibid.*, p. 21.

hastily to a personal and irrational kind of authority.[22] She distinguishes between the kind of leader who inspires strength and confidence in others and the leader with a will to dominate and suggests that charisma is more applicable to inspirational leadership than to the hypnotic leadership which Weber describes.[23]

In view of the confusion about the analytic usefulness of charisma, it is pertinent to ask, what are the relational characteristics between the leader and the led that make the charismatic relationship substantially different from that of caudillos, heroes, and their followers?

Weber provides some guidance here. He defines charisma as the "quality of an individual personality by virtue of which he is set apart from ordinary men and treated as endowed with supernatural, superhuman, or at least specifically exceptional powers or qualities. These are such as are not accessible to the ordinary person, but are regarded as of divine origin or as exemplary, and on the basis of them the individual is treated as a leader."[24] The actual quality of charisma—ethical, aesthetic, or otherwise—is not what gives it validity; the recognition of those subject to its authority is the only requirement for the validity of charisma.[25] Charisma is outside the sphere of everyday routine; it recognizes no abstract rules, no legal principles, no judicial procedure, and no defined spheres of authority.[26] Weber's analysis

---

[22]Dorothy Emmet, *Function, Purpose and Powers: Some Concepts in the Study of Individuals and Society* (London: The Macmillan Co., Ltd., 1958), p. 242.

[23]*Ibid.*, pp. 234–35.

[24]Max Weber, *The Theory of Social and Economic Organization*, trans. A. M. Henderson and Talcott Parsons, edited with and Introduction by Talcott Parsons (New York: Free Press of Glencoe, Inc., 1957), pp. 358–59.

[25]*Ibid.*, p. 359.

[26]*Ibid.*, p. 361.

of the concept of charisma shows that it is the "proph-
etary" quality which distinguishes charisma as a phenomenon from other forms of leadership. If this is essentially the nature of charisma, then it needs to be
studied in the context of alienation, anomie, or other
analysis of withdrawal from one set of norms or in the
examination of the conditions under which another set of
norms becomes acceptable.

Thus there is nothing farfetched in applying the
concept of charisma to the study of politics in the new
states. By and large these states are undergoing rapid
and profound transformation which demands life-style
adjustments on a frightening scale; old norms are falling
into disuse, new ones are beginning to emerge. The unsettling effects of this transformation make the new state
a congenial setting for charismatic politics. However,
since the unsettling effects of rapid social change do not
necessarily lead to alienation or charismatic politics, it
is necessary to inquire more closely into the historical
conditions under which charismatic leaders thrive. On
this point, neither Weber nor those who have employed
his concept of charisma provide adequate guidelines.
As Peter Blau has already pointed out, Weber's theory
"encompasses only the historical processes that lead from
charismatic movements to increasing rationalization and
does not include an analysis of the historical conditions
that give rise to charismatic eruptions in the social
structure."[27]

We suspect that it is the absence of a clear statement of the historical conditions of charismatic politics
that makes it difficult to see through some of the logical
problems that the theory of charismatic legitimation

[27]Peter Blau, "Critical Remarks on Weber's Theory of Authority,"
American Political Science Review, Vol. LVII (1963), p. 309.

seems to pose. Perhaps an example of these logical problems should be given. Weber refers to the followers of
the charismatic leader as a "corporate group" based on
"an emotional form of communal relationship" (*Ge-
meinde*).[28] Thus in a sense charisma implies an "integrated following." The concept of charisma describes a
situation in which different people have identified with
a particular leader and developed a "communistic relationship"[29] through their common involvement in the
mission of their leader. To the extent that charisma
implies an integrated following, the theory of charismatic legitimation offers a purely deductive explanation
of political integration.[30] The theory seeks to explain
how solidarity may be forged among disparate groups;
but it does so by a concept which assumes the existence
of solidarity. It is mainly because of the absence of a
leader or an institution capable of commanding the loyalty of the citizenry of the new state that the problem
of political integration arises in the first place. Since the
theory of charismatic legitimation presupposes the existence of a symbol of national identity—the charismatic
leader—it is a circular explanation of political integration.

It may be retorted that our statement of this logical difficulty ignores the question of scale, that the theory of charismatic legitimation does not argue that the
charismatic leader commands everyone's loyalty; and
further, that even though the appeal of the charismatic
leader may be limited, the fact that it cuts across class
and tribal lines makes it a useful integrative tool.

---

[28] Weber, *op. cit.*, p. 360.

[29] *Ibid.*, p. 361.

[30] Deductive because its *explicans* does not contain statements that go
beyond the *explicandum*. See Karl Popper, *The Logic of Scientific Discovery*
(New York: Basic Books Publishing Co., 1959), pp. 59 ff.

The question of scale is indeed important. The extent of charismatic appeal has to be considered by anyone wishing to make charisma a key variable of a theory explaining how integration can be maximized in a new state. For if in the historical political society to which we wish to apply the theory, there is no leader with a charismatic appeal, the theory is irrelevant. If there is a charismatic leader whose appeal is not extensive enough to be a major lever for stimulating and conditioning mass participation in politics the theory is trivial.

Structural features exist in the new states which generate sentiments that limit the range of people for whom a given person may have charismatic appeal. It is difficult to see how a leader with a nationwide appeal can emerge in the atmosphere of political fragmentation and bitter ethnic rivalries which characterizes most of the new states. Thanks to a crop of excellent case studies of the new states,[31] we know that the nationalist movement tends to be ridden by tensions after the winning of independence: tensions between politicians and intellectuals, the masses and their leaders, urban and rural elements, traditional rulers and westernized elite.[32] These cleavages hamper the emergence of common emotional attitudes.

---

[31]See especially, James Coleman, *Nigeria: Background to Nationalism* (Berkeley and Los Angeles: University of California Press, 1958) ; A. R. Zolberg, *One-Party Government in the Ivory Coast* (Princeton: Princeton University Press, 1964) ; I. William Zartman, *Government and Politics in Northern Africa* (New York: Frederick A. Praeger, Inc., 1963) .

[32]For more on these cleavages, see Edward Shils, "Political Development in the New States," in John Kautsky (ed.) , *Political Change in Underdeveloped Countries: Nationalism and Communism* (New York: John Wiley & Sons, Inc., 1962) , pp. 195–234; James Coleman, "The Problem of Political Integration in Emergent Africa," *Western Political Quarterly*, Vol. VIII, No. 1 (March 1955) , pp. 44–57; W. H. Wriggins, "Impediments to Unity in the New States: The Case of Ceylon," *American Political Science Review*, Vol. LV, No. 2 (June, 1961) , pp. 313–20; and M. Marriot, "Cultural Policy in the New States," in Clifford Geertz (ed.) , *Old Societies and New States: The Quest for Modernity in Asia and Africa* (New York: Free Press of Glencoe, Inc., 1963) , pp. 27–56.

Again, the chance of charismatic leadership lessens after independence. With imperial control eliminated, the aggregation of interest groups which constituted the nationalist movement tends to disintegrate, and the spontaneous enthusiasm of the masses for their leaders begins to wear thin. The leaders are now saddled with the responsibility for governmental failures and social problems. They now assume the unpalatable role of imposing taxes, enforcing law, curbing recalcitrant traditional authorities and disillusioned revolutionaries—and this will impair their popularity. This is hardly the atmosphere for hypnotizing the masses into unquestioning obedience.

Some may well argue that it is precisely such social and political cleavages (and the corresponding political and psychological tensions) that breed charismatic politics. But this only raises the unanswered question of the historical conditions of charismatic phenomena.

Now to some more specific comments on the theory of charismatic legitimation. Apter's identification of Nkrumah as a charismatic leader derives from a rather misleading analogy. Apter states that "most of the effective sources of Nkrumah's charisma have identical functional counterparts as chieftaincy." According to Apter, Nkrumah replaced the chief's authority by meeting the same functional requirements through new social structures.[33] This supposed functional similarity leads Apter to minimize the difficulties of legitimizing the Nkrumah regime.

Assuming that Nkrumah performed the same functions as the chief, would this make him as acceptable as the chief to the ordinary Ghanaian still in the grip of traditional institutions? Does it not matter that these functions were fulfilled through different structures? We

---

[33]Apter, *op. cit.,* pp. 304 ff.

cannot attain sufficient analytic nicety if in the general enthusiasm for functionalism, we allow ourselves to undermine the importance of structures. The sophisticated functionalist will readily admit that the kinds of structures that man the boundaries of the political system do matter, since it is these structures that process the "inputs" and maintain the contact between polity and society.[34] Surely, it makes a difference, politically, whether civic disorder in Alabama is checked by the local police or federal government troops; it matters that the Ashanti peasant now pays his tax to agents of the national government rather than to the vassals of the Asantehene.

So far, we have allowed the assumption that Nkrumah was the functional equivalent of the chief. But what does this mean? Apter himself indicates that Ghana did not have a traditional political system but a multiplicity of traditional systems.[35] The Ashanti system boasted an elaborate bureaucratic government structure, but the Tallensi system was acephalous; the Dagomba has a well-articulated system of chieftaincy, but the Ewe, like the Tiv of Central Nigeria, had an essentially egalitarian system.[36] When we say that Nkrumah is the functional equivalent of the chief, are we referring to the institution of chieftaincy in the context of Ga, Ewe, Moshi, Dagomba, Gonja, Mamprussi, Walla, or Tallensi traditional systems? Since the functions and significance

---

[34]Gabriel Almond, "A Functional Approach to Comparative Politics," in Gabriel Almond and James Coleman (eds.), *The Politics of Developing Areas* (Princeton, N.J.: Princeton University Press, 1960), p. 9.

[35]Apter, *op. cit.*, pp. 81 ff.

[36]To get a picture of the contrast between the Ashanti and Tallensi systems alone, compare K. A. Busia, "The Ashanti," in Daryll Forde (ed.), *African Worlds: Studies in the Cosmological Ideas and Social Values of African Peoples* (Oxford: Oxford University Press, 1954), pp. 190–208, with Meyer Fortes, *The Web of Kinship among the Tallensi* (Oxford: Oxford University Press, 1949), and "The Political System of the Tallensi of the Northern Territories of the Gold Coast," in M. Fortes and E. E. Evans-Pritchard, *African Political Systems* (Oxford: Oxford University Press, 1940), pp. 239–71.

of the chief varied with these systems, it is scarcely meaningful to say that Nkrumah is the functional counterpart of the chief without referring specifically to one of these systems.

Apter has conceded that after Ghana's independence, Nkrumah lost his ability to manipulate the masses.[37] This limited his effectiveness as the instrument of political institutional transfer. In his new book, *The Politics of Modernization,* Apter de-emphasizes the concept of charisma and insofar as he employs it, he makes it a behavioral category rather than a structural one.

But it has been argued that the political experience has tended to validate the theory of charismatic legitimation. For instance, Runciman holds that the routinization of charisma was taking place in Ghana under Nkrumah. Runciman argues that the political instability which the erosion of Nkrumah's charisma was bound to cause was being countered by building up the Convention Peoples Party as a symbol of unity transcending particular governments and persons, and as the incarnation of the aspirations and interests of the people of Ghana.[38] The tendency to regard the dominant party of the new state as an instrument for routinizing charisma is reflected in Irving Horowitz's *Party Charisma.* Horowitz points out that the third world exhibits contrasting trends in the direction of extralegal authority and legal-rational authority; an exaggerated personalism (charismatic leadership) lies side by side with a bureaucratic organization (the party).[39] He suggests that these antithetical tendencies have been synthesized in "party

---

[37]Apter, *op. cit.,* pp. 329–30.

[38]W. G. Runciman, "Charismatic Legitimacy and One-Party Rule in Ghana," *Archives Européennes de Sociologie,* Vol. IV, No. 1 (1963), pp. 148–65.

[39]Irving Louis Horowitz, *Party Charisma,* Studies in Comparative International Development, Vol. I, No. 1 (1965), p. 84.

charisma." With this synthesis charismatic authority is considerably depersonalized and given a less fragile basis. The pressure towards the synthesis is the radical shift in the functions of charisma after the struggle for national liberation. In the revolutionary period, a heightened personal charisma is easily gained by "taking advantage of all the weaknesses of the established social order, by intensifying the mass sense of bewilderment and helplessness without a new set of leaders, and by terrifying the population through the specter of innumerable dangerous enemies."[40] But in the post-revolutionary period charisma tends to become depersonalized as it responds to the need for order and for fusing the "social sectors rendered antagonistic during the revolutionary period."[41]

The idea of party charisma or, what is the same thing, the suggestion that the one-party system is a means of routinizing charisma is interesting and important. It draws attention to one of the serious difficulties of the theory of charismatic legitimation, namely the question as to how the transfer of loyalties from the charismatic leader to the state is to be effected.

Unfortunately, Runciman and Horowitz are not very helpful here. They have shown that in the new states, personalism and bureaucratic structures exist side by side. Horowitz is probably justified in claiming that "the time honored distinctions drawn by Max Weber between the three ways to legitimize authority, through traditionalism, charisma, and rationalism, tend to draw the distinctions more tightly in theory than they are in fact."[42] But the relationship between the two phenomena

---

[40]*Ibid.*, p. 87.
[41]*Ibid.*
[42]Horowitz, *op. cit.*, p. 95.

supposedly synthesized in party charisma still remains obscure. How can the process of routinization be identified?

This is a difficult question. Nevertheless, it can be answered. The problem of finding empirical indicators of the process of routinization can be approached somewhat obliquely through attitude survey research, designed to determine the extent and intensity of the respective appeals of the charismatic leader and the party. A series of such surveys taken at different points in time can be used as an indicator of the shift of loyalties from the charismatic leader to the party or vice versa. Until some way of identifying the process of routinization is found, it will be impossible to realistically evaluate the concept of party charisma in historical terms.

But in the meantime, it must be pointed out that there are indications that the dominant parties of the third world are not so much instruments of routinization as means of reinforcing the authoritarianism of the leader and making his personal influence more pervasive. One may well argue against Runciman's case for the routinization of charisma in Ghana that the last years of the Nkrumah regime were characterized by increasing personal authoritarianism and a growing cult of irrationality rather than by bureaucratization. Endless constitutional amendments, the ritualization of politics, the personification of the symbols of government, unpredictable promotions and demotions, constant cabinet reshuffle, indifference to law, imprisonment without trial —these are some familiar features of Ghana politics during the later years of the Nkrumah regime that readily suggest its antipathy to formal procedure.

The current political history of Africa shows that the downfall of the "national hero" has tended to lead

to the complete collapse of his mass party. The abolition
of Nkrumah's Convention Peoples Party was greeted
with spontaneous demonstrations of support for the National Liberation Council which ousted Nkrumah. Similarly, neither Sylvanus Olympio of Togo nor Fulbert
Youlou of Congo (Brazzaville) was survived by his political machinery. These are indications that the African
mass party exists merely as an element of a simple charismatic condition.

Enough has been said to show that the theory of
charismatic legitimation raises many thorny problems.
To bring the theory nearer to reality and reduce its conceptual difficulties, two modifications must be made.
First the concept of charisma should be dropped, for
while it is not in the final analysis essential to the theory, it is the source of most of the theory's weaknesses.
Reduced to its essentials, the theory of charismatic legitimation suggests that personal authority can further the
legitimation of the new state. The important and interesting thing here is not whether this personal authority
is specifically charismatic but the possibility of an influential personality mediating between the new state
and its citizens. Second, the personal authority which is
to be used for buttressing the state should not be sought
from one charismatic leader but from a multiplicity of
sources—traditional authorities, leaders of important secondary associations, etc. The cultural heterogeneity and
the social and political cleavages of the new state render
unlikely the emergence of a leader with a nationwide
personal appeal and authority.

The usefulness of the theory charismatic legitimation can now be seen in clearer relief. With poignant
simplicity, the theory suggests how integration may be
furthered by exploiting available material—existing loy-

alties. Few will contest the view that the claims of the state are more likely to be accepted if they are put through leaders who can translate them into a language the people can understand and who are influential enough to "sanctify" these claims. Nor will many disagree that this approach to integration is less likely to generate tensions and cause suffering than riding roughshod over existing foci of loyalties. Unfortunately we confront new problems here. How are these influential men to be induced to support the claims of the state? How can they be made to cooperate with one another? We shall return to these questions in a later chapter.

Chapter 5

Political Integration
and the Elite-Mass Gap

This section examines the case for approaching political integration as the systematic bridging of the socioeconomic and cultural "gap" between the ruling elite and the masses. The notion of "the gap," describing as it does a society split on the vertical plane into an upper stratum, which enjoys a monopoly of power and a lower stratum of less privileged people is a familiar one. It reflects the elite-mass dichotomy of sociological theory. Indeed, its roots go beyond sociological theory. It is adumbrated in Plato's tripartite hierarchy of sociopolitical organization and in Aristotelian political theory.

We also discern this dichotomy in the political thought of Machiavelli,[1] for whom the building and maintenance of a nation depend on the creative genius of the great leader—the leader who comprehends the working of social and historical forces and in the light of his knowledge manipulates the masses in order to

---

[1]Machiavelli is best known by his *The Prince*. But anyone who wants to appreciate his insight into political integration will do well to study closely his *Discourses on Livy* and *History of Florence*.

ensure the survival and prosperity of political society despite the vicissitudes of "Fortuna" and the frailties of human nature.

After Machiavelli, this elitism became a prominent feature of European political theory. Elitism pervades the writings of Michels, Mosca, and Pareto. Unlike Machiavelli, these writers were not directly concerned with the problem of integration. They were concerned, rather, with a diagnosis of the ebb and flow of social forces, the possibilities of controlling them, and the consequences of these forces for social organization. It is not surprising that their work yields—at least in an inferential way—useful insights into the problem of political and societal integration. For instance, Mosca's concept of "social types" and his analysis of the causes for their proliferation and the repercussions of such proliferation on the maintenance of stability deserve the careful attention of the student who wants to know why society holds together. So does his exposition of the qualities of the "political class" and the "political formula" and their relation to political stability and national identity.[2]

For our present purpose, we shall confine ourselves to an analysis of the writings of Edward Shils. For Shils, the political integration of the new state depends primarily on the closing of the elite-mass gap. Shils is not the only writer on the new states who recognizes the urgency of bridging this gap. Indeed, practcially every serious student of the political development of the new states recognizes that the socioeconomic (and sometimes even cultural) differences between the masses and the

[2]Gaetano Mosca, *The Ruling Class (Elementi de Scienza Politica)*, trans. Hannah D. Kahn (New York: McGraw-Hill Book Co., Inc., 1939), esp. pp. 70–118.

elite is a real obstacle to the achievement of national identity. But no one has examined the elite-mass gap as systematically and as comprehensively as Shils.[3]

In an article published in 1958, Shils argued that it is mistaken to assume that the gap between the highly political outlook of the ruling elite and the prepolitical outlook of the masses is caused by the detribalization of the former. He pointed out that the advanced modernization of the elite cannot be the relevant point because in its political orientation, the educated elite displays a striking affinity with the traditional cultures from which it is supposed to be emancipated.[4] This affinity lies in the notion that there is a "concentration of charisma in those who rule the nation" and that "the only truly respected motives are those generated by authority."[5] Leaders on the national level are imbued with a sense of the charismatic nature of their authority partly because they tend to regard themselves as instruments of the "spirit of the nation." The masses also associate authority with charis-

---

[3]Coleman and Rosberg define political integration in terms of the elite-mass gap: "Political integration . . . refers to the progressive bridging of the elite-mass gap on the vertical plane in the course of developing an integrated political process and a participant political community." James Coleman and Carl Rosberg, *Political Parties and National Integration in Tropical Africa* (Berkeley and Los Angeles: University of California Press, 1964) , p. 7.

Fortunately, they do not use this narrow concept alone to approach the problem of integration. For them, political integration is only part of a broad subsuming process, "national integration," which also includes "the reduction of cultural and regional tensions and discontinuities on the horizontal plane."

Leonard Binder, "National Integration and Political Development," *American Political Science Review*, Vol. LVII, No. 3 (September, 1964) , pp. 622–63, also sees the elite-mass gap as the major aspect of the malintegration of the new state.

[4]Edward Shils, "The Concentration and Dispersion of Charisma: Their Bearing on Economic Policy in Underdeveloped Countries," *World Politics*, Vol. XI, No. 1 (October, 1958) , pp. 2 ff.

[5]*Ibid.*

ma, although they respond not to authority on the national level, but to the traditional sources of authority—lineage heads, priests, and so on. The tendency to invest authority with charisma leads to the concentration of initiative in the hands of rulers and to passive acquiescence by the rest of the population.

In a later work,[6] Shils points out that one of the factors causing the elite-mass gap is parochialism. He observes that the importance of parochial loyalties in the political and administrative systems of the new states hampers the establishment of a tradition of bureaucratic impartiality. Government officials and political leaders are usually expected to cater to the interests of their kinsmen, rather than to the general welfare. A government regarded as the captive of special interest groups is unlikely to command the loyalty of the citizenry.[7] Again, the prevalence of favoritism generates unnecessary suspicion of the motives of the government. To avoid being discriminated against, interest groups seek to optimize their power position through political action. The result is a proliferation of political organizations. The government that emerges in these circumstances tends to be an uneasy coalition of "segmented and rivalrous interests."

The mutual alienation of the masses and the ruling elite caused by parochialism is according to Shils deepened by the stratification system of the new state. The virtual absence of a substantial social stratum of skilled industrial workers and supervisory rural labor to mediate between the powerful and wealthy on the

[6]Edward Shils, "Political Development in the New States," *Comparative Studies in Society and History*, Vol. II, No. 3 (April, 1960), pp. 265–92; No. 4 (July, 1960), pp. 379–411.

[7]*Ibid.*, pp. 264–70.

one hand and the poor, underprivileged masses on the other leaves the society dangerously polarized. This polarization is perpetuated by an occupational distribution which concentrates such an intermediary social stratum as exists in the urban areas. The fact that this social stratum is isolated from the mass of peasants limits its effectiveness to mediate between, and integrate, the masses and their rulers.[8] The alienation of the masses from their rulers is exacerbated by the fact that the masses are for the most part uneducated in a society in which education is highly valued, not only for its vocational utility but also for the mystique of modernity it confers.[9] Uneducated in such a society, the masses feel inferior and isolated.

The gap is further dramatized by the physical disparity between the towns, with their paved streets, modern office buildings, electricity, and water supply, and the undeveloped countryside lacking the most fundamental social amenities. Furthermore, the isolation of the masses is deepened by their silence and passivity. This passivity has two main causes. First, there was an absence of an infrastructure of voluntary associations (on the village level) geared to aggregating and articulating rural interests. Second, the rural population was socialized into a system in which authority was hierarchical and sacral—a system that gave them no conception of their rights as citizens.[10]

This is undeniably a very thoughtful formulation of one of the major problems of nation-building. No one can deny that there is a concentration of initiative in the hands of the ruling elites of the new states. Nor will anyone quarrel with the suggestion that this con-

---

[8]*Ibid.*, p. 272.
[9]*Ibid.*
[10]*Ibid.*, p. 281.

centration of initiative in a few hands can in certain circumstances lead to the alienation of the masses from their leaders. It is doubly fortunate that Shils should make us conscious of this polarization in the new state. In the first place, this consciousness should prevent us from accepting too hastily the claims of the leaders of the new states that their countries are completely mobilized behind them. Second, it should compel a reappraisal of the intensive politicization of the masses, in which the leaders of the new states are engaged. If it is true that this deep-rooted mutual alienation exists, then the politicization of the masses may conceivably lead to violent class conflict.

Let us turn to Shils's suggestions for bridging the gap. Shils's insight lies more in the solutions he rejects than in the cures he prescribes. His observations on the possibilities of using "nationalist sentiment" or charismatic leaders to achieve political integration are very telling. He grants that charismatic leaders are useful for uniting people who would otherwise have no common identity and for serving as a surrogate for the deficiencies of the political machinery. Nevertheless, he does not think that we should look to them to cure cultural pluralism and political fragmentation, for charismatic leaders leave behind them legacies that may be difficult to assimilate and a leadership vacuum that may be difficult to fill. In addition, charismatic leaders (oriented as they are to personalistic politics and aware that bureaucratization erodes their influence) do not ordinarily build the institutions on which political society must ultimately depend.[11]

Shils is equally skeptical of the possibility of promoting political integration by manipulating national-

---

[11]Shils, "Political Development in the New States," p. 288.

ist sentiments. He argues that the parochialism of the
constituent ethnic groups of the new state retards the
growth of nationalist sentiment. Nationalist sentiment
exists only among the "detribalized" (i.e., the westernized). But even here, it exists only as an ideology. Nationalism overcomes parochialism only "transiently" in
a crisis atmosphere. More still, extreme nationalism in
a culturally pluralistic society could precipitate secessionist movements.[12]

The prescription which Shils offers for bridging
the gap follows logically from his diagnosis of the causes
of the gap. He suggests that the gap be bridged by the
dispersion of initiative. This demands a profound social
and psychological transformation of the masses. The
masses are to be transformed from passive, overdepen-
dent, and fatalistic subjects of authority to articulate,
independent-minded, and dynamic citizens.[13] The pre-
conditions for effecting this transformation are the intense politicization of rural life and a massive program
of universal education designed to widen the individual's cognitive map and to give him the knowledge and
confidence to participate fully in the life of the community. Shils's solution for bridging the gap may be
summed up in two words—political democracy. It is only
political democracy that can guarantee the dispersion of
initiative. It is political democracy that will arouse and
liberate the latent capacities of the masses.

It is difficult to subscribe to the view that political
democracy entails the dispersion of initiative. True,
democracy presupposes—at least in theory—ability and
willingness on the part of the citizenry to participate in
the political process, and on the part of their leaders,

---

[12]*Ibid.*, p. 283.
[13]Shils, "The Concentration and Dispersion of Charisma: Their Bearing
on Economic Policy in Underdeveloped Countries," p. 19.

acceptance of the principle of government by consulta-
tion and consent. But these conditions of political democracy can be met without dispersing initiative. Nothing prevents a democratic community from deciding
(democratically) to concentrate initiative in a few hands.
In spite of Rousseau, people cannot be "forced to be
free." Indeed, in a very real sense, democratic participation amounts to little more than the choice of the
few on whom initiative is to be concentrated.

And what are the chances of institutionalizing political democracy? Shils finds that the polarized nature
of the new state is conducive to an oligarchic political
system. Yet, the gap cannot be bridged by such a political system. An oligarchy, Shils argues, may obscure or
exploit the gap, but it cannot eliminate it. The panacea
for the gap is political democracy. Yet, the gap prevents
the development of political democracy. So a dilemma
is framed. We need political democracy to bridge the
gap, but the very existence of the gap makes political
democracy impossible.

The elite-mass gap is admittedly an important aspect of the malintegration of new states. But it is only
one of the cleavages that beset the new states—and not
demonstrably the most important. It is unfortunate that
emphasis on the elite-mass gap has tended to obscure
the divisions and antagonisms on both sides of the gap.
"Mass" and "elite" are not necessarily homogeneous en-
tities. For instance, those whom we lump together as
the Nigerian masses may be Hausas, Ibos, Yorubas or
Tivs, Catholics, Protestants, Muslims or Animists, peasants or urban laborers. Unless we break down "elite"
and "mass" to their constituent elements we cannot fully
appreciate the complexity of the problem of political
integration. The point can be briefly illustrated with
Shils' argument that ethnic parochialism deepens the

elite-mass gap. Shils argues that the irresistible pressures of ethnic loyalties has made nepotism a prominent feature of public life in the new states; that this increases the alienation of the masses from their leaders because these leaders are regarded as representatives of tribal and familial intrests rather than as champions of the public good. This argument is sound as far as it goes. But there is another side to the matter. Surely, if ethnic parochialism is as pervasive as Shils indicates, we cannot capitalize on the elite-mass gap. A political system in which tribalism constitutes the main force in political life will be characterized not so much by an elite-mass cleavage on the vertical plane, as by a pattern of political alignments cutting across socioeconomic strata on the horizontal plane. In other words, the units of political competition will be coalitions of men from disparate social classes, united by tribe. If this is the case, one could argue that far from causing the mutual alienation of the elite and the masses, ethnic parochialism prevents the masses and their leaders from drifting apart.

We are unlikely to come up with a realistic approach to the problem of political integration if we fail to give meticulous attention to the study of the elites who enjoy a monopolistic control of the politics of the new states.[14] As Shils has shown, the masses of the new

---

[14]Some of the most illuminating studies of the elites of the new states are Peter Lloyd, "Cocoa, Politics and the Yoruba Middle Class," *West Africa,* January 17, 1953; J. E. Goldthorpe, "An African Elite," *British Journal of Sociology,* Vol. VI (March, 1955), pp. 31–47; K. Little, "The African Elite in British West Africa" in A. W. Lind (ed.), *Race Relations in World Perspective* (Honolulu: University of Hawaii Press, 1955), chap. xii; Hugh Smythe, "The Nigerian Elite," *Sociology and Social Research,* Vol. XLIV (September–October, 1959), pp. 42–45; James O'Connell, "The Political Class and Economic Growth," *The Nigerian Journal of Economic and Social Studies,* Vol. VIII, No. 1 (November, 1966), pp. 129–40; and Immanuel Wallerstein, "Elites in French-Speaking West Africa: The Social Basis of Ideas," *Journal of Modern African Studies,* Vol. III, No. 1 (May, 1965), pp. 1–33.

states exist on a level of consciousness that does not fully comprehend the idea of the nation-state. Being predominantly illiterate and unused to political organization more complex than the tribe, the masses of the new state are at a loss to understand the idiom of modern politics. Hence they invariably find themselves reduced to passive subjects of authority.

In these circumstances, political competition becomes essentially an intra-elite struggle. A leader supported by a handful of influential men and a small body of well-organized followers has relatively little difficulty maintaining himself in power.

But power is as easily lost as it is easily acquired. Intense intra-elite competition against the background of an immature political culture renders the new state politically unstable. The immaturity of the political culture means that there are hardly any generally recognized restraints on the methods by which political power may be sought or exercized, and hence a tendency towards extraconstitutionalism. The elitism of the political system means that the political competitor has only few opponents to beat in order to acquire control of the government.

It is not surprising that the governments of the new states are so easily overthrown. If we examine the recent instances of the overthrow of governments in the third world, especially Africa, we see that these governmental changes were results not of popular uprisings but of "palace revolts." For the most part, these governmental changes were accomplished by the elimination of a handful of key political figures. On January 15 (and 16), 1966, Nigeria's federal government was toppled by the assassination of the federal Prime Minister, Alhaji Tafawa Balewa; the federal Minister of Finance, Chief Festus Okotie-Eboh; and two regional

Premiers, Ahmadu Bello and Chief Samuel Akintola. A few months later on July 29, 1966, the new government was in turn overthrown by the assassination of the Ibo leaders of the ruling military junta. Compared to other African coups d'etat, Nigeria's two coups were bloody. The more usual pattern is to arrest the leading politicians and "detain" a handful of their lieutenants.[15] This was what happened in Algeria, June 19, 1965; Congo (Leopoldville), November 25, 1965; the Central African Republic, January 1, 1966; and Upper Volta, January 3, 1966. This is also to some extent true of the Congo (Brazzaville) coup of August 15, 1963. Army leaders and trade-union leaders secured the resignation of President Fulbert Youlou after three days of demonstrations organized by the trade unions; later President Fulbert Youlou was arrested and detained. In the case of the Dahomey coup of December 22, 1965, the military junta did not even bother to detain the leading politicians.

The ascendancy of the military elite does not in fact mean the end of the intense elite competition in the new states, although being specialists in the use of violence the military has a great advantage over other elements in the elite for consolidating its power. To begin with, most of the armies of the new states are too technologically primitive and too numerically small to prevail against well-organized, widespread civilian revolt. Nigeria, a country of 55 million people, boasts an army of only 8,000 men; the Central African Republic has a population of 1,229,000 people but an army of only 450 men. Dahomey has an army of 1,000 and a population of 2,000,300; Togo's population is 1,642,000

---

[15]One other exception is the coup in Togo, January, 1963. President Sylvanus Olympio was assassinated.

but it can only muster a force of 250 men; Upper Volta has a population of 4,400,000 men but an army of only 1,200.[16] The difficulties of maintaining a military regime are compounded by the fact that the military cannot significantly increase its size and coercive resources without imposing a severe strain on the economy—a strain that may well accelerate its downfall. Again the military of the new state tends to reflect its social tensions. After the second coup of July 29, 1966, the Nigerian army disintegrated along tribal lines, a factor that weakened the federal government. Tribal tensions within the Congolese army are making it increasingly difficult for General Mobutu to maintain his grip on the Congo.

To all appearances the ultimate cure for the inherent instability of the new states lies mainly in the modification of the political behavior of its elites. As long as they are so avowedly elitists and so bitterly contentious, their political power will always be precarious. The dangers of a sudden loss of power and its unpleasant consequences can be expected to put pressure on the elite to temper their competitiveness and to support mass participation and constitutionalism.

If it is allowed that politics in the new states is essentially elitist and that the political loyalties of the masses are largely determined by ethnicity, then we may postulate that the political stability (and to some extent the political integration) of the new state is greatly furthered by increasing the group-cohesiveness of its elites.

As we pointed out earlier, a situation in which ethnic particularism is the major force in politics will pro-

[16]These figures are taken from *Africa Report*, Vol. II, No. 2 (February, 1966), pp. 12–13. Algerian and Congo (Leopoldville) have somewhat larger armies. Algeria has an army of 50,000 and population of 10,300,000; and Congo (Leopoldville) an army of 29,000 and a population of 14,000,000.

duce a pattern of political alignments cutting across the socioeconomic strata and hence preventing the mutual alienation of the rich and the poor. Further, since the masses are assumed to follow their leaders somewhat passively in this segmentary system of political alignments, a major condition of political stability is the progressive reduction of the difference between the leaders (elites) of the different segments.

Unfortunately, the problem of political integration is not necessarily simplified by reducing it to one of increasing elite-consensus. Even though tribalism may be the main force in the politics of the new state, it does not follow that the political elite of the new state can simply be identified with its tribal leaders.[17] There are other loyalties—e.g., professional and religious—which sometimes compete with tribal loyalties and hamper the cohesiveness of the elite.

What is characterized as the elite of the new state, is usually an aggregation of disparate "social types." It includes the westernized urban middle classes, intellectuals, businessmen, professional men such as lawyers, army officers, and the higher echelons of the civil service. It includes the traditional oligarchy—the powerful chiefs and members of the more prestigious vocations of traditional society such as the marabouts—who are for the most part nonwesternized. It also includes the semiwesternized middle classes such as contractors, wealthy farmers, and entrepreneurs.

---

[17]For an example of the problems of defining the elite in the new states, see T. Hodgkin, "The African Middle Class," *Corona,* Vol. VIII, No. 3 (1956), pp. 85–88; P. Morton-Williams, "A Discussion of the Theory of Elites in a West African (Yoruba) Context," in "Proceedings of the Fourth Annual Conference of the West African Institute of Social and Economic Research," March, 1955 (mimeographed), University College, Ibadan, 1956; Martin Kilson, "Nationalism and Social Classes in British West Africa," *Journal of Politics,* Vol. XX (May, 1958), pp. 368–87.

The goals and interests of these different groups within the elite are sometimes incompatible. For instance, the westernized elite cannot carry out a thoroughgoing policy of industrialization without impinging on the interests of the traditional authorities.

The integration of the different elements of the elite of the new state is by no means an easy task. We shall return to this problem in the final chapter. For the moment, it should be emphasized that the amelioration of the malintegration of the new state demands not so much the bridging of the elite-mass gap as the progressive reduction of the tensions within the political elite.[18]

---

[18]These tensions have been examined in Chapter 2. See also Manfred Halpern, *The Politics of Social Change in the Middle East and North Africa* (Princeton, N.J.: Princeton University Press, 1963) , pp. 60–67.

Chapter 6

Unipartyism and
Political Integration

The leaders of the single-party states of the third world have developed an elaborate body of theories to justify unipartyism.[1] Unipartyism, it has been argued, is at once stabilizing and integrative; it reflects the legacy of government by consensus characteristic of most traditional political systems and prevents the dissipation of energy in desultory political strife.[2] Julius Nyerere of Tanzania maintains that the task of throwing off the colonial yoke and eradicating ignorance and poverty "calls for the maximum united effort by the whole coun-

---

[1]Following James Coleman and Carl Rosberg, *Political Parties and National Integration in Tropical Africa* (Berkeley and Los Angeles: University of California Press, 1966), we shall refer to the idea of the one-party state as unipartyism.

[2]For the body of arguments justifying unipartyism, see Madeira Keita, "Le Parti Unique en Afrique," *Présence Africaine*, No. 30 (February–March, 1960); Julius Nyerere, *Ujama: The Basis of African Socialism* (Dar-es-Salaam, 1962); Nyerere, "One-Party Rule," *Spearhead* (Dar-es-Salaam, November, 1961); Sékou Touré, *La Lutte du Parti Démocratique de Guinée pour l'Émancipation Africaine* (Conakry: Imprimerie Nationale, 1959); Kwame Nkrumah, *I Speak of Freedom* (New York: Frederick A. Praeger, Inc., 1962), especially pp. 161 ff.; and Nkrumah, "What the Party Stands For," *The Party*, Vol. I, No. 1 (1960).

try if it is to succeed." The struggle for political and economic emancipation creates a national emergency which leaves no room for divisions.

In Western democracies, it is an accepted practice in time of emergency for opposition parties to sink their differences and join together in forming a national government. This is our time of emergency, and until our war against poverty, ignorance and disease has been won, we should not let our unity be destroyed by a desire to follow somebody else's "book of rules."[3]

Madeira Keita of Mali maintains that Mali's single party reflects the unity of Mali. Mali, he points out, is not divided by "philosophical, religious or ideological differences; her citizens are animated by common objectives—economic, cultural and social development" and what is needed is a method that will enable the country to carry out these objectives as rapidly as possible:

Now, since our objectives are common ones and we are in agreement on methods, we must create a single party. It is necessary to create a single party to be efficient, to remedy the situation, and not to give aid to the anonymous adversary colonialism which up to the present has been instrumental in the division of our country. We must have the unified party in order to limit the possibilities of corruption and to attempt to destroy opportunism for these constitute dangers that threaten the African parties and the action of the government and parliaments.[4]

Party ideologues are not the only ones who regard unipartyism as an asset to nation-building. There are scholars who see some validity in the claims that have

---

[3]Paul Sigmund (ed.), *The Ideologies of Developing Countries* (New York: Frederick A. Praeger, Inc., 1963), p. 199.
[4]*Ibid.*, p. 176.

been made for single-party systems.[5] Without ruling out the possibility that a "competitive party system in a new state could be the structural arrangement producing the most effective functional performance, as well as the most rapid modernization," Coleman and Rosberg maintain that "it is a fact that in the immediate postcolonial period in many African states, the dominant party seemed to be the national institution most capable of performing a variety of political functions."[6] These functions are specified: interest articulation and aggregation, political recruitment, political socialization, political communication, national integration. They conclude that the party can indeed perform these functions.[7] In particular, they point out that the revolutionary-centralizing single-party systems have helped to ameliorate one kind of malintegration—the elite-mass

[5]For scholarly analysis of unipartyism, see Ruth Schachter, "Single-Party Systems in West Africa," *American Political Science Review,* Vol. LV, No. 2 (June, 1961), pp. 294–307; C. H. Moore, "The Neo-Destour Party, a Structure for Democracy?" *World Politics,* Vol. XIV (April, 1962), pp. 461–82; R. Hinden, "Africa and Democracy," *Encounter,* No. 8 (London, 1962); R. F. Gray, "Political Parties in New African Nations: An Anthropological Viewpoint," *Comparative Studies in Society and History,* Vol. V (July, 1963), pp. 449–61; Henry L. Bretton, "Current Political Thought and Practice in Ghana," *American Political Science Review,* Vol. LII, No. 1 (March, 1958), pp. 46–63; Immanuel Wallerstein, "The Political Ideology of the P.D.G.," *Présence Africaine* (English ed.), Vol. XII (First Quarter, 1962), pp. 30–41; J. A. Torres, "The Political Ideology of Guided Democracy," *Review of Politics,* Vol. XXV (January, 1963), pp. 34–63; R. Emerson, *Political Modernization: The Single-Party System,* University of Denver Monograph Series in World Affairs No. 1 (Denver, 1964); J. G. Liebenow, "The One-Party State in West Africa: Its Strengths and Weaknesses in the Nation-Building Process" in W. H. Lewis (ed.), *French-Speaking West Africa: The Search for Identity* (New York: Walker & Company, 1965), pp. 45–57; Aristide Zolberg, "Mass Parties and National Integration: The Case of the Ivory Coast," *Journal of Politics,* Vol. XXV, No. 1 (February, 1963), pp. 36–48; "Effets de la Structure d'un Parti Politique sur l'Integration Nationale," *Cahiers d'Etudes Africaines,* No. 3 (October, 1960), pp. 140–49; and "One-Party Systems and Government for the People," *Africa Today* (May, 1962).
[6]Coleman and Rosberg, *op. cit.,* p. 657.
[7]*Ibid.,* p. 680.

gap—by their ultrapopulism.[8] Wallerstein posits that the single-party system furthers social solidarity with its ideology and enables integration to be accomplished in a manner which maximizes popular participation. As Wallerstein sees it, the one-party system not only furthers political integration, it is conducive to political stability; African states do not have a choice between one-party systems and multiparty systems but only a choice between "one-party states and either anarchy or military regimes or various combinations of the two."[9] Apter has stressed the interplay of Nkrumah's charisma and the Convention Peoples Party in promoting political institutional transfer in Ghana. According to Apter, the Convention Peoples Party "formed a major element in the societalization of what was a predominantly localized and fragmented set of tribal and regional areas but hitherto without social cohesiveness beyond the tribal purview."[10]

The aim of this chapter is to try to determine whether the phenomenon of unipartyism sheds any light on the problem of political integration. To begin with, it must be remembered that unipartyism is a phenomenon that takes different forms and characters with different social and political consequences. We may for instance distinguish between one-party systems in terms of the pervasiveness of their influences. The Communist party of Russia has completely remoulded Russia's political, economic, and social structures according to its principles; and every aspect of Russian life is impregnated with its influence. On the other hand, the Fascist

---

[8]*Ibid.*, p. 687.

[9]Immanuel Wallerstein, *Africa: The Politics of Independence* (New York: Vintage Books, 1961) , p. 96.

[10]David Apter, *Ghana in Transition* (New York: Atheneum Publishers, 1963) , pp. 212, 304.

party of Italy and the National Socialist party of Germany imposed themselves on existing political structures; they did not completely transform existing social and economic institutions.[11] These two parties were obliged to claim formal rights over other institutions and to establish paramilitary and parapolitical organizations to support themselves. In Russia where the principles of the Communist party permeated the way of life, it was unnecessary to found these subsidiary organizations. We may also distinguish between single-party systems such as the Union Soudanaise of Mali and to some extent that of Guinea which were formed by a merger—largely voluntary—of rival political organizations, and others such as the Convention Peoples Party, established through the systematic coercion of opposing parties. In the short run, single-party systems instituted by coercion are latently unstable because their high-handed measures against their opponents leave a legacy of extra-constitutionalism. For instance the stability of the Nkrumah regime in Ghana was more apparent than real. The high-handedness of his regime was matched by the extra-constitutional methods of his opponents who resorted to bombing public buildings and national monuments and plotting to assassinate leading politicians. So a vicious circle of political extremism was created. In contrast, the opposition to the institution of the single-party system in Tanzania, Guinea, and Mali has been less formidable and less prone to violence.

The differences between single-party systems noted here are only those of degree. However, they are important. For as we have seen, they help to explain the presence or absence of certain institutions and the incidence of violence.

---

[11]Ernest Barker, *Reflections on Government* (New York: Oxford University Press, Inc., 1958), pp. 285–86.

It is thus clear that the question of the relevance of unipartyism to political integration cannot be satisfactorily answered on the level of generality. Account must be taken of the different varieties of one-party states. And an analysis which takes account of these variations may well turn out to be too complex to warrant any generalizations about the relation of unipartyism to political integration.

Yet a general theoretical discussion of the relation between unipartyism and political integration could be illuminating. While single-party systems differ in many respects, they have some common characteristics. If these characteristics are abstracted and clearly stated, the question may be raised whether and in what sense these characteristics affect the level of integration of political systems that possess them. This question is useful because it leads us to explore the correlation between political structures and political integration.

All single-party systems are similar in three major ways. First, every single-party system tends to be "allied with the ideas of the heroic age and the heroic leader. The whole of the party, in each case, professes a 'vocation of leadership' in the nation, for which it finds the example and the inspiration in the single leader who leads his 'following' of leaders."[12] To realize the "ideas of the heroic age" the energies of the masses must be canalized; the masses must be mobilized and guided. As a result, single-party systems tend to be characterized by different combinations of elitism and populism.

Second, every single-party system tends to regard itself as the emanation of the *volksgeist* and as the only accredited representative of all legitimate interests within the nation. The claim that the party concretizes the public interest leads the party to condemn political

---

[12]*Ibid.*, p. 286.

opposition to its rule and principles as a threat to the public good. This claim also puts the party elite under pressure to minimize the political relevance of social differences and to dramatize popular support for its policies.

The single-party system tends to blur the distinction between the political and the social. The party is not content merely to be the main channel of communication between government and society.[13] It seeks to be synonymous with both. Hence it tries to politicize and control every aspect of social life.

These political characteristics affect the level of integration in some important ways. In order to accommodate the multiplicity of interests which it claims to protect, the party must to some extent harmonize them. By acting as a broker among conflicting interests, the party moderates group competition and reduces the possibility of social cleavages leading to serious political conflicts. This balancing of conflicting interests is reflected in the approach of the African single-party systems to industrialization. While the tardy (usually the traditional authorities) are prodded, the impetuous (usually doctrinaire socialists) are restrained. In Guinea, Mali, Tunisia, Tanzania, Kenya, and Algeria, the party leadership has been as much concerned with restraining militant trade unionists and Marxian socialists as with modernizing the rural sector and disciplining extreme traditionalists. In 1963, President Bourguiba of Tunisia personally intervened to expel the radical socialists who had infiltrated and seized control of the influential Paris-

---

[13]This is usually identified as the main function of political parties, particularly in "competitive" political systems. See Avery Leiserson, "The Place of Parties in the Study of Politics," *American Political Science Review*, Vol. LI, No. 4 (December, 1957), pp. 948 ff.; Sigmund Neumann (ed.), *Modern Political Parties* (Chicago: The University of Chicago Press, 1956), p. 397.

based Tunisian youth organization.[14] In 1956, he acted quickly to suppress (and in some cases, conciliate) the radicals who had instigated the revolt of the Union Generale des Travailleurs Tunisiens against him.[15] The Nkrumah regime maneuvered to avoid being captured by right- or left-wing extremists. By 1961, the ascendancy of the radical wing of the Convention Peoples Party had seemed complete. Nkrumah had been encouraged to discredit the right wing and dismiss Kojo Botsio, Ayeh-Kumi, S. Yeboah, and K. Ghedemah.[16] But the balance was quickly restored when in mid-1962 the leaders of the radical wing of the party, Tawia Adamafio, Ako Adjei, and Kofi Crabbe, were denounced and arrested.

The single-party system furthers political integration by perpetuating agreement on the modes of acquisition and exercise of political power. Such agreement minimzes the role of social differences in political life. It is possible for a country to achieve a degree of political integration quite out of proportion to its social homogeneity. "Social differences have meaning in politics only when individuals act on them, using the power resources at their disposal by virtue of social differentiation."[17] For its continued existence and solidarity, every

[14]Douglas E. Ashford, *The Elusiveness of Power: The African Single-Party State,* Cornell Research Papers in International Studies III (Ithaca, 1965), p. 12. For more on the role of single-party systems in maintaining a balance among opposing social forces, see pp. 10–15.

[15]For more on this labor revolt, see Douglas E. Ashford, "The Neo-Destour Leadership and the Confiscated Revolution" in W. H. Lewis (ed.), *French-Speaking West Africa: The Search for Identity* (New York: Walker & Company, 1965), pp. 83–84.

[16]On the ideological undertone of this move, see *Statement by the President concerning Properties and Business Connections of Ministers and Ministerial Secretaries* (Accra: Government Printer, 1961); and Kwame Nkrumah, *Broadcast to the Nation* (Accra: Ghana Information Services, 1961).

[17]Ashford, *The Elusiveness of Power,* p. 14.

coalition, ipso facto, imposes on the power-holders of its constituent elements restraint in the acquisition and exercise of power. But such restraint is particularly necessary in the case of the single-party system which accommodates many disparate interests and poses as the nucleus of a nation united behind its leaders. To the extent that the party elite fails to play down tribal differences, it weakens its own solidarity and threatens political stability. Some single-party systems have made limitations on the exploiting of social differences for political purposes quite explicit. Ghana's Avoidance of Discrimination Act of 1957 forbids the use of racist, religious, or tribal propaganda. In the Ivory Coast the Parti Democratique de la Cote d'Ivoire has openly committed itself to eliminate "racism and ethnic particularism" from political life.[18]

However, the policy of denying political significance to certain social differences cannot be more than moderately successful. The single-party system does not eliminate intra-elite competition but merely concentrates it, and it sometimes happens that the competitors find the temptation to gain a temporary advantage by a subtle appeal to social differences irresistible. Sometimes the diffusion of the dominant party's influence has depended on its ability to appeal to particular social groups, such as underprivileged rural laborers and minority groups like the Hamallists in Mali and the Harrists in the Ivory Coast.[19]

The single-party system furthers integration by increasing political participation and by expanding the perimeter and deepening the intensity of "social communication." Since the party prefers to pose as the re-

---

[18]Aristide Zolberg, "Ivory Coast," in Coleman and Rosberg (eds.), *op. cit.,* p. 87.

[19]Schachter, *op. cit.,* p. 301.

pository of the *volksgeist,* it strives for broad-based support. Unlike the "patron" parties of the early nationalist era, the single-party system is concerned with more than wooing influential people; it fulfills a multiplicity of social needs, pays meticulous attention to political education, and encourages mass participation. The masses must be mobilized to realize the goals of the party and to demonstrate that the whole nation is behind the party elite. Mass participation inculcates the sense of involvement. People whose visions could not go beyond the tribal horizon begin to see that national problems have a claim on their attention. Political participation, in turn, promotes social communication. The single-party system brings together leaders from diverse social and ethnic groups. Because these leaders have to cooperate to direct the state, they are obliged to balance their particularistic interests against competing claims.

On the mass level, participation in the same organization promotes social solidarity not only by facilitating regular interaction among different groups but also by exposing people from different backgrounds to common influences, particularly party ideology. The leadership level is probably better integrated than the mass level because the leaders are more mobile, more ideologically sophisticated, more in contact with other ethnic groups.

Most of the basic organizational units of the party are in the villages. Since villages are for the most part ethnically homogeneous, participation on the village level—and this is the level on which most people participate—contributes little to forging horizontal trans-ethnic links.

To be sure, these horizontal links are to some extent supplied by the auxiliary organizations that the party proliferates. For example, the Convention Peoples Party sponsored the Trade Union Congress, the Ghana

Cooperative Movement, the Workers' Brigade, the Ghana Legion, the Young Pioneers, the National Council of Ghana Women, and the National Association of Socialist Students.[20] The Union Soudanaise of Mali sponsors the Jeunesse de l'Union Soudanaise—Rassemblement Démocratique Africain, the Union des Femmes de Mali, the Union Nationale des Travailleurs Maliens, the Anciens Combattants et Victimes de la Guerre, and the Mouvement Soudanais de la Paix.[21] In spite of its Rousseauian disdain for partial associations, the Parti Démocratique de Guinée maintains the Union Syndicale des Travailleurs de Guinee and the Jeunesse Rassemblement Démocratique Africain.

These associations facilitate contact between the lower echelons of party members in a nonethnic setting. But the contribution of these associations to integration is limited. In the first place, these associations are in a very real sense different permutations of the activities of party militants. Secondly, these associations are predominantly uban phenomena; they reinforce the solidarity of urban dwellers. But they do little to integrate the villagers who are once again likely to participate in these associations on largely ethnically homogeneous organizational levels.

Single-party systems are essentially authoritarian, and there is a sense in which political authoritarianism facilitates the drive for integration. Chapter 2 has shown how cultural and social cleavages and the uncertainty of its political culture threatens the newly independent state with political fragmentation. This threat is compounded by the drive for political integration. As will be shown later, the drive for integration, involving as

---

[20]Apter in Coleman and Rosberg (eds.), *op. cit.*, pp. 293–99.
[21]Hodgkin and Morgenthau in Coleman and Rosberg (eds.), *op. cit.*, p. 246.

it must a massive social transformation, is bound to aggravate the psychological confusion of the transitional
society and to impinge on powerful interests. The attempt to transfer loyalties from the tribe to the state is
likely to be resisted by traditional authorities anxious
to preserve their influence and by minorities fearful of
being permanently subordinated to the larger tribes;
moves to increase economic integration may be resisted
by the wealthier regions fearful of becoming their broth-
ers' keepers. It is hardly surprising that the movement
for national unification has led to secessionism in many
new states such as Ghana, Kenya, Nigeria, Uganda,
Sudan, and Congo (Leopoldville). To guarantee a minimum of stability in the presence of these centrifugal
forces, a powerful government is required. The power
of the government must be sufficiently concentrated to
enable it to act quickly and decisively. There is some
truth in Julius Nyerere's claim that the process of nation-
building creates an emergency which calls for authoritarianism.

However, it is arguable that the authoritarianism
of most single-party states is so thoroughgoing that it
defeats the purpose of preventing political fragmentation. Since the party monopolizes the coercive machinery of the state and alone decides who gets what, every
interest group naturally strives to maximize its influence
within it. In a sense the party's omnipotence makes political competition more bitter than it would be if there
were other loci of power, other important vehicles of
resource allocation.

As Arthur Lewis suggests, unipartyism makes politics a zero-sum game.[22] It stimulates a type of political
competition in which the stakes are exceedingly high.

---

[22]Arthur Lewis, "Beyond African Dictatorship," *Encounter*, Vol. XXV,
No. 2 (August, 1965), pp. 3–18.

It is win all or lose all. In such competition there is a strong urge to seek victory by every available means, little prudence in abiding by the rules of the game. And where there are no restraints on political competition, there is little hope for stability.

Let us carry this point about stability one step further. Since the party equates itself with the state and the nation, it considers organized political opposition to its rule mistaken and illegitimate. This means that dissenters are not allowed to articulate their views outside the party structure. Consequently, political opposition assumes the form of clandestine organizations, now and then surfacing with violent eruptions. Unipartyism perpetuates power monopoly and forces political dissenters to take desperate measures. This in turn provokes the regime to apply extreme sanctions, and a vicious spiral of political extremism is set in motion. An atmosphere in which political arguments can only be settled by imprisonments, bombs, or *coups d'état* is not conducive to the growth of constitutionalism, the hallmark of stability. Unipartyism thus endangers stability and impedes integration by discouraging the growth of that mutual self-restraint which makes the coexistence of different interests within the same political society possible.

Exponents of unipartyism may riposte that the question of giving political opposition legal channels of expression is irrelevant, that the party not only represents every interest but also encourages internal democracy, which makes it unnecessary for dissenters to resort to extraconstitutional measures. It may well be that the single-party system practices internal democracy. However, this is beside the point. The crux is that there may be people who reject, in principle, the single-party system. Some intellectuals of the new states, such as

K. A. Busia of Ghana, find the one-party system ideologically distasteful and conducive to irresponsible dogma-
tism. It is pointless to remind such people that the party
is essentially democratic because in their view, this is
a claim that the one-party system qua one-party system
cannot make.[23]

Clearly, this general theoretical analysis yields nothing conclusive about the relation of unipartyism to political integration. To determine whether on balance,
unipartyism promotes or retards integration requires a
closer examination of the integrative and the disintegrative effects of unipartyism outlined here. This in turn
calls for a detailed examination of a wide variety of historical single-party states. Yet, it is unnecessary to settle
the issue one way or the other. Our limited purpose
here was to determine whether from an analysis of
the phenomenon of unipartyism some insights may be
gleaned for formulating a general statement about the
political structures and the political ethos most conducive to furthering integration.

It has been shown that some characteristics of single-
party systems such as political authoritarianism and the
propensity to politicize every aspect of social life and to
render social differences politically irrelevant are to some
extent positively associated with political integration. In
the final chapter it will be shown at greater length why
political systems that possess these political characteristics are more likely to achieve greater integration than
those that lack them.

---

[23]By the very fact that it denies legitimacy to competing political
organizations.

Chapter 7

Political Integration, Societal Change, and Political Stability

A GENERAL THEORY

It is time to pull the strands together. We have examined different aspects of and approaches to the problem of political integration. With the help of the insight gleaned from this exercise, we shall now attempt to formulate a statement about the conditions under which the drive for greater integration is most likely to succeed.

In the introductory chapter, we defined the problem of political integration in the new states broadly as follows: how to build a coherent political society from a multiplicity of "traditional societies," how to increase cultural homogeneity and value consensus, and how to elicit from the individual deference and devotion to the claims of the state. We argued that in the final analysis, the primary prerequisite for a high degree of integration is a mature political culture, political culture being defined as "the system of empirical beliefs, expressive

96

symbols and values which defines the situation in which political action takes place."[1] We further argued that the essential preliminary for the emergence of a mature political culture in the new states is the broadening and intensifying of "social communication."

To improve its communicative facilities, the new state must undertake social mobilization—"the process in which major clusters of old social, economic and psychological commitments are eroded or broken down and people become available for new patterns of socialization and behavior."[2]

Social mobilization entails the breaking down of physical barriers between people and facilitating a greater flow of goods and services between the different parts of the country, educating the masses, developing urban centers and the mass media, etc.[3] Involving as it does a massive transformation of old ways of life, social mobilization generates tensions. Those whose power is eroded in the process may seek to destroy the new order. Those obliged to leave their folk culture may become lonely and insecure and inclined to doubt the meaning of their new life. Such loneliness and insecurity tend to breed alienation and extremist political movements.[4]

We confront a paradox here. To increase its political integration, the new state must undertake social

---

[1]Sidney Verba, "Comparative Political Culture," in Lucian Pye and Sidney Verba (eds.), *Political Culture and Political Development* (Princeton, N.J.: Princeton University Press, 1965), p. 513.

[2]Karl Deutsch, "Social Mobilization and Political Development," *American Political Science Review*, Vol. LV, No. 3 (September, 1961), p. 494.

[3]For what social mobilization entails, see Deutsch, *ibid.*, pp. 493–514.

[4]See Melvin Seeman, "On the Meaning of Alienation," *American Sociological Review*, Vol. XXIV (December, 1959), pp. 789–90; and Erich Fromm, *The Sane Society* (New York: Rinehart & Co., 1955), p. 110.

On the relation between alienation and social movements, see Hadley Cantril, *The Psychology of Social Movements* (New York: John Wiley & Sons, Inc., 1941).

mobilization. Yet social mobilization is essentially disruptive of the political order in the short run. The problem of political integration in the new states is thus reducible to two related questions: What characteristics must the political system possess to enable it to undertake social mobilization effectively? What type of political system is most capable of neutralizing the disruptive short-run effects of social mobilization? Or to put it another way, how can a minimum of political stability be maintained in the face of the disruptive effects of social mobilization?

Before attempting to answer these questions, it is necessary to examine the meaning of political stability and its relation to social change.

The structure of a political system is the concatenation of its component units and the relations between them. The minimal unit is the individual political actor, and the maximum unit is the political system as a whole. Between these two limits are the complex units or subsystems (political parties, the legislative assembly, the electoral district) which are configurations of the minimal unit.

A political system is said to be stable when the exchanges, that is, the inputs and outputs between its component units (minimal and complex) and between it (the system) and its environment are regular enough to make possible the persistence of the main structural pattern of the system. The flow of exchanges is regular when it takes place within a framework of commonly held beliefs regarding what constitutes legitimate responses and expectations in the context of political interaction, that is, when it takes place within an institutionalized normative culture.

However, the mere existence of a normative culture

is not by itself the sufficient guarantee of a predictable pattern of exchanges. Political actors must be largely committed to acting according to the expectations and responses legitimized by the normative culture. To the extent that such commitment exists, the flow of exchanges is insulated against "erratic" variations that tend to disrupt the political structure.

The relation between political stability and political integration is clear. Political stability depends on the existence of and commitment to a normative culture regulating the flow of exchanges within the political system and between the system and its environment.[5] Political integration depends on the existence of and commitment to a political culture regulating political behavior. So while political stability and political integration are not synonymous, they both essentially depend on the same thing. It is not surprising that the more integrated political systems are also the more stable.

It may seem paradoxical that a study concerned with political change should be employing the techniques and vocabulary of structural-functional analysis. For it has been objected that structural-functional analysis stresses the static to the neglect of the dynamic because it hinges on the concepts of equilibrium and system.[6] Further, it has been argued that as long as we orient our analysis towards the functioning of a suppos-

---

[5] It is not assumed that the normative culture regulating the exchanges within the system is the same as the normative culture regulating the exchanges between the system and its environment. Such an assumption is wrong and unnecessary to the argument.

[6] For a criticism of structural-functional analysis, see David Lockwood, "Some Remarks on 'The Social System,'" *British Journal of Sociology*, Vol. VII (1956), pp. 134–46; Ralf Dahrendorf, "Out of Utopia," *American Journal of Sociology*, Vol. LXIV (1958), pp. 115–27; and Wayne Hield, "The Study of Change in Social Sciences," *British Journal of Sociology*, Vol. V (1954), pp. 1–10.

edly coordinated system, "then the representatives of society as a system is the last point of reference,"[7] and we limit ourselves to determining the "intentional" and "unintentional" consequences of the component units of the system for the preservation of the system.

Nevertheless I think that far from impeding our understanding of the process of change, the structural-functional description of how the system holds together enhances it by providing us with a point of departure for the analysis of change.[8] It is somewhat misleading to say that structural-functional analysis assumes the stability of the main structural patterns of the political system. What is assumed is that both the system and its environment are so continually subject to disruptive forces that the main structural pattern of the system cannot be maintained unless there is some means for compensating for the impact of these forces. No one claims that all the processes that go on within the political system are necessarily equilibrating, that is, conducive to system maintenance. On the contrary, it is recognized that some of the processes that go on within the system are dysfunctional, that is, conducive to the disruption of the system.

Indeed, we may define political stability and the change of political structures in terms of these two processes. We may say that the political system is stable

---

[7] Ralf Dahrendorf, "Toward a Theory of Social Conflict," in Amitai Etzioni and Eva Etzioni (eds.), *Social Change: Sources, Patterns, and Consequences* (New York: Basic Books Publishing Co., 1964), p. 102.

[8] Talcott Parsons, "Some Considerations on the Theory of Social Change," *Rural Sociology*, Vol. XXVI, No. 3 (1961), pp. 219–38, is an elegant example of how functional approach can illuminate the process of change. Related: Francesca Cancian, "Functional Analysis of Change," *American Sociological Review*, Vol. XXV, No. 6 (1960), pp. 818–26; and Ernest Nagel, "A Formalization of Functionalism," in his *Logic without Metaphysics* (New York: Free Press of Glencoe, Inc., 1956), pp. 247–83.

when the impact on the system of the dysfunctional processes generated by the system and the environment are neutralized to the extent of keeping them from altering, in the main, the structure of the political system. On the other hand, structural political change occurs when in any particular instances dysfunctional processes overbalance equilibrating processes thereby causing adjustment of the structural pattern of the political system. If the dysfunctional processes are of such magnitude that no amount of structural adjustment can preserve the main structural pattern of the political system, the political system disintegrates.

We shall now attempt to describe the type of political system that is most capable of undertaking social mobilization and of neutralizing the dysfunctional processes that social mobilization unleashes.

Our theory is that the political system undertaking social mobilization maximizes its capacity for carrying out the process and remaining stable despite the potentially disruptive short-run effects of social mobilization if it is authoritarian, paternal, "identific," and consensual. If any of these four structural characteristics is absent and to the extent that functionally compensating factors are also absent, the destabilizing effects of social mobilizations are increased.

These four structural characteristics—authoritarian, paternal, "identific," and consensual—will be briefly discussed in an attempt to show how they give the political system the resiliency for absorbing change. An attempt will also be made to give them operational meaning so that we may be able to determine whether any given historical political system possesses them. Each of these genetic structural characteristics will be resolved into a set of empirical questions. The questions listed under each characteristic do not necessarily exhaust its empirical indicators. These sets of questions are meant to be demonstrative rather than exhaustive.

1.   *Authoritarian*

A political system is authoritarian[9] if the government's power is large, concentrated, and easily mobilized, and if the government manifests a determination and ability to use this power to carry out its policies.

Power may be defined as ability to change things, in particular, ability to get somebody to do a thing he would not otherwise do.

Power is a relation. It is always exercised by something or somebody (subject) on another person or thing (object) for the achievement of a given goal.

In analyzing a power relation, it is helpful to make distinctions between the sources of power, the means of exercising power, and the response that the exercise of power evokes. These analytic distinctions must not be maintained too rigidly because all three aspects of power are in reality inseparable. We learn very little about power if we simply identify its source. For unless this power base is somehow exploited, it is strictly speaking not power. Again, even when we identify the source of power and the means for its exercise, we still do not fully understand a power relation until we are able to determine the response that it evokes because the most tangible evidence of the existence of power is the response that it evokes.

In analyzing the power of a government over its

---

[9]To avoid confusion, the reader should try to forget for the moment the notion that authority is a special case of power.

citizens, one may identify these three aspects of power as follows: the source of government power may be the esteem of the citizens for the government, the economic resources and information that the government commands, the government's constitutional rights, etc.; the means for exercising government power may be the army, the police force, the civil service, the mass media, etc.; response to the government's exercise of its power may be enthusiastic, reluctant, oppositional, etc.

This conceptual framework reveals the limitations on the power of the government of the new state. It was pointed out earlier that one of the crucial aspects of the problem of political integration in the new states is the task of eliciting from the individual respect for the state and deference to its claims. The new states are still in the process of winning their legitimacy. To the extent that they do not command the loyalty of their citizens, they are denied access to an important source of state power and reduced to relying mainly on coercion for carrying out their policies.

Again, the power of the new state is limited by the meagerness of the economic resources at its command. Of course, the meager economic resources of the government of the new state may become an important source of power in a society that boasts very few private fortunes. Even when due allowance is made for this possibility, it remains clear that the meagerness of the economic resources of the government of the new state limits its ability to influence the behavior of its citizens and to change the environment in which they live.

The capabilities of the government of the new state for exercising its potential power are similarly limited. Most of the new states suffer from a shortage of coercive personnel. This point has already been made in an earlier chapter where we compared the numerical strength of the military and the population of various African states. As a means for exercising government power, the civil services of the new states manifest obvious weaknesses. Some of them are barely recovering from the administrative confusion caused by the transfer of power from the colonial rulers to an indigenous government. Many of the men who man the higher echelons of the civil service are new men in new positions and are still unsure of their new roles. The acceptance of bureaucratic norms and the enforcement of government directives are impeded by tribal parochialism. The grip of the government on the citizens is limited by the poor communications network linking the different parts of the country.

The problem is not that the governments of the new states are too powerful but that they are too powerless. It is mainly because their power is so limited that they have been only moderately successful in accomplishing the changes to which they are committed. Quite clearly then, the government of the new state must have more power if it is to accomplish the massive changes which social mobilization calls for.

But it is not enough for the government to command a large amount of power. This power must be highly concentrated. Unless power is so concentrated, it cannot always be easily mobilized. A government that can easily mobilize its power increases its maneuverability; it enhances its ability to apply the requisite pressures in the relevant places at the time when these pressures are likely to be most effective; above all, it can act with greater speed to control the centrifugal forces that social mobilization will activate.

If we are correct in identifying the relative absence

of an institutionalized normative culture as the explanation of the malintegration and political instability of the new state, then it is easy to see that the new state cannot afford to be democratic particularly if it is intent on social mobilization. Democratic diffusion of power implies a high degree of political integration which in turn presupposes a mature political culture. Democratic diffusion of power presupposes the existence of internalized and institutionalized restraints on political behavior, potent enough to prevent the different pockets of power in the political system from destroying one another (and the state) through uninhibited self-assertiveness.

EMPIRICAL INDICATORS:

1. Are political resources (i.e., means of gaining political power, such as money) concentrated in a few hands?
2. Is the social structure such that the influence of the political class is cumulative? In other words, does control over political resources give them control over other resources?
3. Is the coercive personnel of the government large, loyal, and effective?
4. Is interest articulation largely limited to suggestion of policy alternatives within the government structure?
5. In the light of the division of power in the constitution, is the central government strong in relation to regional and local governments?
6. Is the power of the central government highly concentrated in a few hands and institutions?
7. Can the central government easily sidetrack the constitutional checks on its power?
8. Does the central government manifest a determination to decide quickly and act decisively?

2.   *Paternal*

A political system dominated by a political class that is willing and able to lead is paternal.

The leaders of the new states must not only concentrate power in their own hands, they must also father the transformation of their societies. To the extent that they are seriously committed to the integration of their culturally pluralistic societies, these leaders are "innovating" leaders.[10] To integrate they must change—on a massive scale. They must destroy or modify certain habits of mind and undermine certain traditional symbols of collective identity; they must induce the people to accept new norms, new goals, new motivations; they must readjust long-established patterns of social and economic relationships. They are in effect introducing a way of life that is quite alien to their people. They must supply the initiative for realizing it. Inevitably, politics takes on a paternalistic tone.

In the present context paternalism implies not only an oligarchic concentration of initiative but also the willingness and ability to lead. The unsettling effects of social mobilization will breed uncertainty and anxiety.[11] People in the grip of anxiety may seek therapy in extremist mass movements or sink into defeatist apathy. Political leaders have to give their followers confidence

---

[10]This analytic distinction is borrowed from Carl Freidrich, "Political Leadership and the Problem of Charismatic Power," *Journal of Politics,* Vol. XXIII, No. 1 (February, 1961) , pp. 3–24.

[11]On the causes and political consequences of anxiety, see Franz Neumann, "Anxiety and Politics," in Herbert Marcuse (ed.) , *The Democratic and the Authoritarian State: Essays in Political and Legal Theory by Franz Neumann* (New York: Free Press of Glencoe, Inc., 1957) , pp. 170–95; and Harold Lasswell, "The Psychology of Hitlerism," *Political Quarterly,* Vol. IV (July–September, 1933) , pp. 373–84.

Related: Ann Willner and Dorothy Willner, "The Rise and Role of Charismatic Leaders," *Annals of the American Academy,* Vol. CCCLVIII (March, 1965) , pp. 77–88.

and a sense of purpose and help them to find coherence and meaning in their new life. Ideological movements can help the citizens of the new state to solve the problem of existential identity which they face by giving meaning to their past, a perspective on the present, and hope for the future.

While the political class should monopolize power, it should attempt to imbue the masses with a sense of having some control over their lives. The appearance of mass participation in the decision-making process must be kept up with great care for, as we have seen, a general feeling of helplessness tends to precipitate alienation. Besides, social mobilization aims at changes of such magnitude that its success depends largely on the cooperative effort of the whole society. Voluntary support is to be preferred to coerced support because it is usually more enthusiastic and cheaper. But voluntary support is likely to be obtained by a political class that makes the rest of the population feel that they are impotent subjects of the authority of the political class.

Empirical Indicators:

1. Does the "output of messages" from the government outweigh the "input of messages" from society?[12]
2. Are associational interest groups controlled by the political class?
3. Do political leaders see themselves as "fathers" of the nation?
4. Has the political class been able to devise some means (e.g., an ideology) for giving their followers a central perspective on life?

---

[12]Gabriel Almond, "A Functional Approach to Comparative Politics," in Gabriel Almond and James Coleman (eds.), *The Politics of Developing Areas* (Princeton, N.J.: Princeton University Press, 1960), p. 17.

3. *Identific*

This word has been coined to describe a political system characterized by mutual identity between the political class and the governed. A political system is identific to the extent that—

a) There is a free flow of communications between the political class[13] and the governed.
b) The "political formula"[14] of the political class is acceptable to the governed. (Political formula is the principle—moral, legal, philosophical, etc.—on which the government's claims to political power rest.)
c) The civic body considers that it has some interest in the continued existence of the government.

Communication facilities are an important instrument of government power. The existence of channels of communication between the political class and the governed enhances the government's ability to influence the behavior of its citizens.

But it is not enough to be concerned with the possibilities of transmitting the government's directives to the governed. There is also a need for channels for transmitting ideas and information from the people to the political class. In the first place this helps to give the governed some sense of having some control over events and to neutralize their tendency to feel helpless and alienated. But just as important is the fact that this upward flow of ideas and information helps the political class to understand the governed. By understanding the

---

[13]The term is from Gaetano Mosca.

[14]This term is also from Gaetano Mosca. For more on these terms, see Gaetano Mosca, *The Ruling Class (Elementi di Scienza Politica)*, trans. Hannah D. Kahn, ed. by Arthur Livingston (New York: McGraw-Hill Book Co., Inc., 1939) , pp. 50, 70.

fears, the beliefs, the interests, and life expectations of
the governed, the political class is better equipped for
determining what incentives to offer, what superstition
to exploit, and what pressures to apply to mobilize support for its policies. A government that understands the
governed in this sense has less need for coercion and consequently eliminates some of the tensions of social mobilization.

It goes without saying that all things being equal,
a government that relies exclusively on coercion is far
less powerful—i.e., far less able to influence the behavior
of its citizens—than a government that commands not
only coercive force but also voluntary support deriving
from popular acceptance of its political formula. The
malintegration and relative impotence of the new state
is partly due to a lack of a well-articulated and widely
accepted political formula.

The coming of independence has in some sense
tended to weaken the political solidarity of the people
of the new state because the elimination of the common
enemy—the colonizers—tends to dramatize the differences
between the disparate groups that united in the anticolonial movement. This increases the problem of legitimizing the power of the political class. The leaders of
the new state are still grappling with this problem.
Partly because of these intellectual limitations, their attempts to start ideological movements have been rather
clumsy. By and large the political ideologies they have
formulated have tended to be extensions of their cult
of personality; the result is that the acceptability of
these ideologies has varied with the personal popularity of their proponents.

The problem of winning legitimacy is exacerbated
by the fact that the claims of the political class to the

loyalty of the people have to compete with the claims of the traditional authorities and also by the fact that the political class is obliged to put forward the claims of a modern state to a people who do not fully understand the idiom of modern government.

But the pull of the traditional way of life does not always work to the disadvantage of the political class. For one thing, ethnic particularism helps to make the political system more identific by helping to produce a pattern of segmentary political alignments cutting across the elite-mass gap, and thus keeping the political system from being dangerously polarized.

One way by which the political class can enhance its legitimacy is to convince the governed that the government serves their interest. Here, it is the belief rather than the reality that counts. It may be that in reality, the government may not be serving the interest of the governed. But as long as the governed somehow believe that the government serves their interest, the legitimacy of the government is enhanced.

To be sure, this does not relieve the government of the responsibility of striving to promote the public welfare. It must have some concrete achievements to point to because if belief and reality diverge too widely people may begin to ask embarrassing questions. True, men do not live by bread alone. But then men eat before they believe. The political class must demonstrate that investment of individual loyalty in the state pays off.

Unfortunately this is easier said than done. The resources at the command of the new state are too meager to enable it to offer utilitarian incentives to "integrative behavior" on the scale that is needed. Nor is the new state in a position to effect dramatic changes in the physical environment of its people in the short run.

EMPIRICAL INDICATORS:

1. Is the "political formula" of the ruling elite widely accepted?
2. Is the incidence of anomic interest articulation low? Note that a low incidence of anomic interest articulation is not always indicative of mutual identity of rulers and the ruled; it may also be an indication that the government is severely repressive.
3. Are there cultural symbols and historical experiences that can be exploited for reinforcing social solidarity?
4. Is there a general feeling that political leaders are not enjoying an unduly large share of the economic rewards of the system?
5. Is there a general feeling that the political leaders are diligent and honest servants of the public interest?
6. Are there channels for quick and effective transmission of information between the political class and the governed?

4. *Consensual*

A political system is consensual if the political class is solidary and if the hegemony of the political class is not threatened by a counter-elite.

To keep political class solidary, policies should be formulated in a way that will win the broadest possible support within this class; there should be an efficient mechanism for conflict resolution and enforcement of discipline within this class; emphasis should be placed on the collective responsibility of the political class.

To keep the political class free from the threat of being displaced by counter-elites entails co-opting into the political class everyone who controls an important base of power. The political class should be a coalition of the leaders of the major social, religious, professional, and ethnic groups. For if any of these major groups considers its interest underrepresented and adopts an antagonistic attitude towards the political class, a counter-elite is created in the leaders of this dissenting group.

Perhaps we can clarify our concepts of a consensual political system by contrasting it to a one-party system. The idea of elite-consensus proposed here bears a closer resemblance to Weber's "party of notables" than to the one-party systems of the new states. In our scheme, consensus is sought not at the grass-root level but at the leadership level by enlisting the support of leading personalities from all major social groups. The government is sustained by the influence of the leading personalities loyal to it. These leaders mediate between the government and society.

In contrast to this, the one-party system seeks consensus at all levels of society; that is one reason why it places so much emphasis on politicizing the masses. Support for the government depends not so much on the personal influence of its leading personalities as on the ability of the party machinery to mobilize the masses; hence the passion for organization and discipline.

The advantages of a consensual political system are obvious. To begin with, the fact that the government represents the major interests reduces the chances of its being regarded as an instrument for promoting particularistic (as opposed to public) interests. This, in turn, enhances the government's ability to win popular loyalty and hence its power.

Again, a consensual political system will tend to minimize the politically divisive effects of social differences. It is possible for a country to achieve a degree of political stability quite out of proportion to its social homogeneity. Social differences are particularly politically divisive when people begin to exploit them.[15] The elite coalition will be obliged to impose restraints on the modes of acquisition and exercise of political power for the simple reason that if its members exploit social differences without restraint, the coalition cannot be solidary or effective, and the state over which it presides may disintegrate. So elite-consensus is invaluable for reducing the political importance of social differences and taking some of the fierceness out of political competition.

EMPIRICAL INDICATORS:

1. Are there strong disincentives (coercive, economic, etc.) to factionalism within the ruling elite?
2. Is every major social, ethnic, and religious group adequately (i.e., in terms of numerical strength, economic power, etc.) represented in the government?
3. Is there a symbol (e.g., a charismatic leader, an ideology) which commands the loyalty of the ruling elite?
4. Is the number of influential people openly hostile to the government small (in relation to the number of influential people openly supporting the government)?
5. Is there a machinery for resolving conflict within the ruling elite? Are the decisions reached by means of this machinery generally respected and accepted?

Our theory suggests that divergence from or approximation to the paradigmatic political structure described

[15]Douglas E. Ashford, *The Elusiveness of Power: The African Single Party State* (Ithaca: Center for International Studies, Cornell University, 1965), p. 14.

here is the factor that explains the failure or success of historical political systems undertaking social mobilization. To test it, we must have the means for identifying empirically the data subsumed under each of our four main concepts. Unfortunately, we have met this requirement only in a limited sense. The indicators suggested by the empirical questions under each of these four concepts operationalize them only in a crude sense. Some of these questions need to be broken down into subquestions before their "operational" utility can be maximized. What is more, the indicators we have do not pretend to exhaust the operational meaning of these concepts.

It would be desirable not only to have an exhaustive list of indicators but also to construct a scale for each set of indicators and to devise some means of converting the observed structural features of historical political systems into scores so that a high score will point to the existence of a great amount of what it is that we are measuring. A further refinement would be the construction of an overall scale combining the items on the respective scales of the four analytic concepts.

While these theoretical niceties would have given our theory greater precision and perhaps the air of scientific respectability, we have reluctantly decided to forego them. We felt that emphasis on operationalism would have forced us to reformulate our key concepts in a way that would have made them less useful for understanding the problem to which this study is addressed. We also felt that we could not give priority to precision and measurability without leaning too heavily on easily measurable data which may not necessarily be the most relevant to the research problem.

It is sufficient for our purposes if our discussion of our key concepts makes pragmatically clear the nature of the empirical data relevant to each concept. To put it more concretely, while we have not exhaustively enumerated all the empirical indicators of authoritarianism nor supplied the means for measuring it with mathematical precision, we have defined it with sufficient rigor to enable the researcher seeking to test the theory to recognize the general nature of the data subsumed under the concept.

Perhaps a few words should be said about the testability of theories, particularly the type of theory advanced here. In general, theories may be tested by the following criteria:

1. The extent to which the theory is a logical response to the research problem.
2. Internal consistency of the theoretical system.
3. Whether the logical form of the theory is empirical (i.e., such that the theory can be refuted by phenomenal experience) or metaphysical (i.e., such that the theory cannot be refuted by phenomenal experience) .[16]
4. Empirical applications of the hypotheses derived from the theory. (In particular, experimental results must be consistent with the predictions of the theory.)

The first two tests are indeed important. But their importance can easily be exaggerated. There may be many logical responses to one problem, so the first criterion is not very helpful for choosing between competing theories. The limitation of the second criterion is

[16]See Karl Popper, *The Logic of Scientific Discovery*, Harper Torchbook Edition (New York: Harper & Row Publishers, Inc., 1965) , pp. 32–33.

that a rigid insistence on internal consistency sometimes leads to an overgeometrized conceptual framework without the requisite flexibility for coping with the world of experience.

The third criterion is entailed by the fourth and will not be discussed separately. The difficulties of testing a theory of societal change by the fourth criterion are obvious. First, there is the difficulty of making precise predictions due to the complexity of the subject matter with which the theory deals. Second, there is the uncomfortable fact that hypotheses derived from entirely different theories may be supported by the same phenomenon. Third, and most important, is the impossibility of experimentation under highly controlled conditions. It is impossible to make observations of political systems under the highly controlled conditions of the physics laboratory.

This does not mean that the type of theory advanced here is totally untestable by the all-important fourth criterion. To experiment is to make observations under controlled conditions.[17] Experimentation is precise comparison in the sense that its interest lies in knowing what observable differences are made by a given alteration in the experimental conditions. A theory of societal change can be tested by a cruder kind of comparison. One can compare the behavior of the political systems of historical societies that underwent (or are undergoing) rapid and massive change. If what we learn of the experience of these political systems is consistent with the theory advanced here, then the theory is to some extent corroborated. If we fail to establish such consistency, the theory is falsified.

---

[17]A. R. Radcliffe-Brown, *A Natural Science of Society* (Glencoe: Free Press of Glencoe, Inc., 1948) , p. 37.

THEORY AND HISTORICAL EXPERIENCE

The experience of certain historical societies will now be examined in the light of the theory. The aim of this exercise is to determine whether and to what extent historical political societies which survived an "integrative revolution" or the destabilizing impact of rapid social change exhibited the structural characteristics prescribed by the theory. While the following analysis of historical data does not pretend to supply proof of the empirical validity of the theory, it increases its testability by supplying in terms of the theory, "falsifiable" propositions about the experience of certain historical political systems.

We shall begin by looking at the United States of America. What emerged after the anticolonial revolution was in Washington's words a "half-starved limping government." The government could make treaties, issue currency, and borrow money, but little else; it had virtually no coercive personnel to enforce its laws. The Philadelphia Constitution improved the prospects of holding the country together. But when Washington became President in 1789, under the new Constitution, the prospects of preserving the Union were still rather slim. The new Constitution had been ratified by very narrow margins in several states, and it was evident that some sections of the country, such as the commercial East and the agrarian South, were deeply suspicious of one another. Nearly all the states were still jealously guarding their autonomy. There was "an unknown but fearful burden of debt, almost no revenue, and a prostrate credit."[18]

---

[18]Leonard White, *The Federalist: A Study in Administrative History* (New York: The Macmillan Co., 1956), p. 1.

During her "integrative revolution" in the four
decades after 1787, the political system of the United
States manifested to a considerable degree the four
structural characteristics of our theory. The paternal
element was very much in evidence. The movement for
"a more perfect Union" was not a response to popular
demand but the initiative of several leading personalities such as Washington, Franklin, the Morrises, John
Marshall, Hamilton, the Pinckneys, Madison, Rufus
King, and James Wilson. The Federalist party—if indeed we may call it a party—was not a mass party but
an organization linking notables from different parts of
the country. Unquestionably, Federalist leaders considered that their leadership was absolutely necessary for
the survival and prosperity of the young nation.[19] They
were "Founding Fathers" in every sense. By and large,
"Federalist policies were based on Hamilton's view that
governments had to be ruled by gentlemen, by his dis-
trust of popular majorities and by his conviction that
American progress depended upon bringing the wealthy
and the well-born to the firm support of the new government."[20] Professor Schattschneider reaches much the
same conclusion when he writes that the "Federalists
sought to perpetuate the power of a relatively small
group of men of position and property who were therefore opposed to efforts to organize the masses."[21] He ar-

[19]For more on the paternalism of Federalist leaders, see John Roche,
"The Founding Fathers: A Reform Caucus in Action," *American Political
Science Review*, Vol. LX (1961), p. 801.

[20]Morton Grodzins, "Political Parties and the Crisis of Succession in
the United States: The Case of 1800," in La Palombara and Myron Weiner
(eds.), *Political Parties and Political Development* (Princeton, N.J.: Princeton
University Press, 1966), p. 305.

[21]E. E. Schattschneider, "United States: The Functional Approach
to Party Government," in Sigmund Neumann (ed.), *Modern Political Parties:
Approaches to Comparative Politics* (Chicago: University of Chicago Press,
1956), p. 195.

gues that it was in order to avoid inviting a challenge
to the supremacy of the Federalist obligarchy that the
Federalists developed antiparty ideas.

In *An Economic Interpretation of the Constitution,*
Charles Beard tries to show that the Constitution of 1789
reflects the interest of an economically privileged oligarchy which led the Federalist party. He points out
that a vast majority of the delegates at Philadelphia represented the most powerful economic interests such as
the slave owners of the South, manufacturers and ship-
pers, lawyers, bankers. Partly because an overwhelming
majority of the delegates held government bonds, they
had a strong interest in a strong federal government.[22]
As Charles Beard's critics have suggested, it may well
be that the convention did not always act as a "consolidated group," that property interests did not entirely
shape the new constitution.[23] But whatever their ulterior
motives, the Federalist party leadership was an economically and socially privileged group, convinced of its
ability to lead.

Federalist leaders never pretended to be other than
"upperclass Americans who had a natural-born right to
rule their inferiors in the social and economic scale."[24]
They believed that "the aim of every political institution is, or ought to be first to obtain for rulers men who
possess most wisdom to discern, and virtue to pursue

---

[22]Charles Beard, *An Economic Interpretation of the Constitution of the United States* (New York: The Macmillan Co., 1943), esp. pp. 52–63.

[23]Charles Warren, *The Making of the Constitution,* disputes the view that property interests shaped the Constitution; Forrest MacDonald, *We the People* (Chicago: The University of Chicago Press, 1958), finds that the delegates at Philadelphia did not act as a cohesive interest group. For an-other critical look at the Beard thesis, see Robert Brown, *Charles Beard and the Constitution* (Princeton: Princeton University Press, 1956).

[24]John C. Miller, *The Federalist Era 1789–1801* (New York: Harper & Bros., 1960), p. 109.

the common good of the society."[25] And if it so happens that these virtues are found among the "rich and well-born" should they not "have a distinct and permanent share in the government"?[26]

From what has been said already, it can be inferred that the political system was not highly identific. The aristocratic contempt for the common man of Federalist leaders such as Alexander Hamilton and John Adams was quite open. They had no intention of giving any significant political power to the masses who in Hamilton's words, "seldom judge or determine right."[27] They tended to the view that in the mass, men are capricious, malicious, and disorderly, and this led them to disdain "the vile love of popularity"; they would not "truckle to the people" even when their political office was at stake.[28]

It is hardly surprising that in the period under survey, political participation was systematically limited. It has been estimated that not more than 3 percent of the adult male population took part in the election of the delegates to the ratifying conventions. The Philadelphia convention agreed that for the purposes of taxation and the apportionment of seats, all free inhabitants of the country were to be counted. But it was unable to extend the franchise to all free inhabitants of the country. The question of the franchise was left to the states who imposed property qualifications. Direct election was allowed only in the case of the House of Representatives. Electoral colleges in the states elected the

---

[25]Edward Mead Earle (ed.), *The Federalist: A Commentary on the Constitution of the United States* (New York: The Modern Library, 1937), No. 57 (Hamilton or Madison), p. 370.

[26]Hamilton, quoted by Louis M. Hacker, *Alexander Hamilton in the American Tradition* (New York: McGraw-Hill Book Co., Inc., 1957), p. 115.

[27]*Ibid.*

[28]Miller, *op. cit.*, p. 133.

President who in turn appointed judges; the Senate was chosen through the state legislature. This system of indirect elections was apparently a device for insulating the political system against "vulgar" influences.

Apathy, ignorance, and the unsettling effects of the ever-moving frontier helped to keep the disenfranchised —mainly slaves, small shopkeepers, debtors, mechanics, frontiersmen—from organizing to maximize their influence on the government. The remoteness of the national government from the ordinary people was increased by the poor physical communication. The improvement of communications facilities was impeded by "strict constructionists who narrowly interpreted the powers of the national government under the constitution."[29]

The identific element was further weakened by the limited appeal of the political formula of the Federalist oligarchy. The political formula of the Federalist oligarchy stressed the advantages of "a more perfect union" to all Americans. It was argued that as long as the country was a loose aggregation of squabbling states it could never be a first rate power, nor could it command the respect of other nations. "Weakness and divisions at home would invite dangers from abroad."[30] A strong federal government would reduce internal friction and provide greater security for everyone. Popular acceptance of the political formula was limited by the aloofness of the Federalist oligarchy from the masses. It is difficult to say whether the Federalist leaders would have succeeded in getting this political formula generally accepted by the people even if they had made a more strenuous effort to propagate it. The common man may

---

[29]Marian D. Irish and James W. Prothro, *The Politics of American Democracy* (Englewood Cliffs, N.J.: Prentice-Hall, Inc., 1959), p. 129.

[30]*Federalist* No. 5 (Jay), p. 25. See also No. 4 (Jay), pp. 17–22, and Nos. 6 and 7 (Hamilton), pp. 27–40.

well have asked embarrassing questions as to who bene-
fited from the suppression of slave revolts and the Shay's
rebellion. Perhaps it should be noted that the political
system did not become significantly more identific with
the ascendancy of Jefferson. Jefferson had no intention
of precipitating a participation explosion. The most influential supporters of Jeffersonian Republicanism were
the slave-owning aristocratic families of Virginia who
despised the brashness and vulgarity of the *nouveaux
riches* of the Eastern seaboard. Such people were hardly
in a position to talk too loudly about democratic participation.

The weakness of the identific element must not be
overemphasized. There were some redeeming features,
such as the absence of language barriers, the common
background of European culture, the charismatic appeal
of George Washington, and the common experience of
the anticolonial war.

Despite the rivalry among the leading politicians
and the different states, the American political system
was considerably consensual. Charles Beard's analysis has
shown that all the powerful economic interests had a
compelling reason for supporting a strong federal government. John Roche points out that nearly all the
delegates at the Constitutional Convention were supporters of a strong federal government and that the differences that plagued the convention were tactical rather
than ideological.[31] During its ascendancy, the Federalist
party was supported by the industrialists of the North,
most of the press, the Chambers of Commerce, the
professional classes, the New England Congregational
Churches, and for a time, the wealthy farmers of the
South. The new constitution was worked by its ardent

---

[31]Roche, *op. cit.*, pp. 804 ff.

supporters in its early years. In the election of 1788, the Federalists gained almost total control of both federal legislative houses; only Virginia returned Anti-Federalist senators.

The rivalries within Washington's cabinet may have tended to obscure the extent to which the American political system was consensual in the decade after 1789. Washington's charismatic appeal and undisputed power drastically reduced the disintegrative impact of these rivalries on the political system. His prestige was "so great that he commanded the loyalty of the leaders of the different factions as well as the general populace."[32] It is telling that despite the growing influence and restlessness of the Jeffersonians, the choice of Washington for a second term was unanimous.

As might have been expected, when Washington retired from the presidency, elite-consensus rapidly broke down. The coalition of northeastern businessmen and influential southern farmers on which Federalist power was based during the party's ascendancy could not last. These two elements within the Federalist party stood to gain by supplanting the Confederation with a federal constitution. But they had little else in common. It was difficult for the new government to devise economic policies that could satisfy their often divergent interests. This became increasingly evident after 1790 when Hamilton launched his fiscal and economic policies. By 1792 the conflict of interests had already crystallized into political parties.

By the end of the decade the rivalry between the Federalists and the Republicans had grown so bitter

---

[32]Seymour M. Lipset, *The First New Nation: The United States in Historical and Comparative Perspective* (New York: Basic Books Publishing Co., 1963), p. 23.

that there was danger of a violent showdown. Let us identify some of the events that led to this situation.[33] First, the Whisky Rebellion of 1794. This was an armed rising of the farmers of western Pennsylvania and neighboring Virginia against the federal tax on distilled liquor. Washington put down the rebellion with 13,000 troops. The intervention of the federal government embittered the Republican agrarians who were distrustful of a strong federal government, particularly one dominated by "stock holders and bank directors." Another source of conflict was the Jay Treaty made between the United States and Britain in 1795 during the Anglo-French war. Jefferson's party was infuriated by the treaty which they regarded as a betrayal of the spirit of 1776. Yet another cause of bitterness was the Alien and Sedition Laws of 1798. These laws extended the period of residency required to qualify immigrants for citizenship from 5 to 14 years; the President was authorized to deport aliens deemed dangerous to domestic peace and national security; heavy penalties were to be imposed on anyone who spoke or wrote anything deemed to disparage Congress or the government. It was apparent that this body of legislation was aimed at stifling the Jeffersonians. Some of the leading pamphleteers of the Republican party were recent immigrants; so were many of their supporters. The Sedition Laws were used to harass the Republican press. Some of their minor newspapers were forced to cease publication. Suit was brought against leading Republican publications such as the *Aurora,* the *Independent Chronicle,* and the *Argus.* There were other causes of bitterness such as

---

[33]My account relies heavily on Professor Morton Grodzins' excellent summary of these events. See Morton Grodzins in La Palombara and Weiner, *op. cit.,* pp. 307–12.

the Virginia and Kentucky Resolutions and the Fries Rebellion of 1799. But we shall not dwell on these. These events generated so much tension and so much bitterness that the survival of the Union after the 1800 election seemed doubtful.

It is indeed rather surprising that the transfer of power of 1800 was accomplished without the breakdown of the political system or even widespread violence. I think the explanation is that the breakdown of elite-consensus was not as complete as it seemed. The High Federalists who favored systematic liquidation of the opposition were clearly in the minority; they were strong only in a few places like Massachusetts and Connecticut. In spite of their revolt against the ticket, Adams and Pinckney did well. They lost narrowly (63 to 75) to Jefferson and Burr. Both Adams and Jefferson were committed to moderation and the preservation of the Union. In refusing to share the enthusiasm of the Hamiltonians for war against France, Adams was taking much the some position as Jefferson on the most pressing issue of foreign policy. Indeed, as Professor Grodzins has pointed out, Adams' behavior indicates that he had greater confidence in Jefferson's ability to lead the nation than in Hamilton's.[34] The American political system survived 1800 essentially because it was considerably consensual.

We already have indications that the American political system was highly authoritarian in the period under survey. Popular participation in the decision-making process was drastically limited. William Miller estimates that of 3,250,000 people (excluding American Indians) in the United States at the close of the Revolution, over one million were "unfree." Among the "unfree" were

---

[34]Morton Grodzins in La Palombara and Weiner, *op. cit.*, p. 321.

600,000 Negro slaves, 300,000 indentured servants, some 50,000 convicts who had no legal standing because they had entered the country illegally, a few thousand vagrants, and debtors subjected to forced labor by court order. Another million women who were neither slaves nor servants had few legal rights. Married women could neither hold property nor will it; women could not hold public office. The states that had "inadvertently" given the vote to women proceeded to disenfranchise them.

According to Miller, by the mid-1780's no more than 400,000 free adults could be found in the United States, and because some of these people were busy battling the wilds of the frontier, they had little time for politics.[35] "All told, at the close of the revolution, perhaps 120,000 Americans could meet the property, religious or other qualifications to vote. . . . Fewer still could hold office."[36]

The United States was in effect a one-party system for over four decades. The Federalists had dominated the system until 1800, when power shifted to the Jeffersonians. Even then, a two-party system did not really emerge because the Federalist party was crippled by the growing popularity of the Republican party and the intraparty splits of 1796–1800. We may get an idea of the extent of Jefferson's personal dominance from Adams' complaint that "there was scarcely an attempt made in the Senate for seven years to oppose anything he desired."[37] When Jefferson left office he personally designated Madison as his successor; this was to be the pattern of presidential succession for the next two dec-

---

[35]William Miller, *A New History of the United States* (New York: Dell Publishing Co., 1962) , pp. 104 ff.

[36]*Ibid.*, p. 106.

[37]Schattschneider, *op. cit.*, p. 196.

ades. "From 1809, when Madison took over from Jefferson, each President was followed in office by his chief cabinet officer, the Secretary of State. And a national two-party system did not emerge until the 1830's when Jackson's opponents united in the Whig Party."[38]

Not only was the political structure authoritarian, the tone of politics was also markedly authoritarian. Hamilton argued for a "Governor" of the United States elected for life. The governor was to appoint state governors who were to have absolute veto over state laws. The Federalists were unfavorably disposed towards party competition. Washington talks of "the daemon of party spirit."[39] Madison inveighs against "the pestilential influence of party animosities—the disease most incident to deliberative bodies and most apt to contaminate their proceedings."[40] For Hamilton, the Jeffersonians were always "disorganizers" and "Jacobins." On the whole the Federalists tended to view organized opposition as "seditious . . . and treasonable."[41]

Within the limits of this cursory survey of the relevant historical evidence, we have tried to determine the extent to which the American political system exhibited the four structural characteristics of our theory during her "integrative revolution." We have seen that the political system was markedly consensual, paternal, and authoritarian. In particular, its consensual structure gave it the resiliency to survive the crucial elections of 1800.

---

[38]Lipset, *op. cit.*, p. 44.

[39]J. C. Fitzpatrick (ed.), *The Writings of George Washington* (Washington, D.C., 1931–44), Vol. XXXI, p. 48.

George Washington's farewell address is a good example of his distaste for party politics.

[40]*The Federalist*, No. 37 (Madison), p. 232.

[41]Marshall Smelser, "The Federalist Period as an Age of Passion," *The American Quarterly*, Vol. X (1958), pp. 394 ff.

The identific element was weak, as we have seen, but there were compensatory factors which prevented a slave revolt.

Stalinist Russia is not an example of a political system driving for integration. Nevertheless it is relevant to our theory because it is an example of a political system that survived social and economic change of staggering proportions and pulverizing momentum. An idea of the scale of the adjustments that the Russian people had to make may be obtained by contemplating Stalin's achievements. Within a period of 16 years (1924–40) the cultivated land increased by 74 percent, steel output was multiplied by 18, coal production by 10, engineering and metal industries by 150, industrial output by 24, and annual capital investment by 57.[42] The agrarian revolution consolidated roughly 25,000,000 family plots into about 250,000 kolkhozes.[43]

During this period, the political structure of Russia was conspicuously authoritarian. There was universal franchise, but this did not mean that power was widely diffused because there was only the party slate to vote for. The bulk of the population did not belong to the party which was avowedly an elite organization. Within the party, power was concentrated in such organs as the Organization Bureau, the Secretariat, and the Politburo (which were nominally subordinate organs of the Central Committee) and the Central Committee. These organs were in turn dominated by Stalin. By 1929 he had emerged as the undisputed victor from the power strug-

---

[42]See Frederick L. Schuman, *Soviet Politics: At Home and Abroad* (New York: Alfred A. Knopf, Inc., 1946), p. 212. I have relied heavily on Professor Schuman's excellent writings on Russia.

[43]On the impact of these changes, see Maurice Hindus, *Men and Politics* (New York: Duell, Sloan & Pearce, 1941); Walter Duranty, *Duranty Reports Russia* (New York: Viking Press, Inc., 1934).

gle that had divided the party since Lenin's last years. He deposed Tomsky, the leader of the trade unions, and Rykov, the premier; Trotsky was expelled from Russia, and Bukharin, the leader of the Communist International, was relieved of his post and ousted from the Politburo. By 1930, Stalin had become in Isaac Deutscher's words, "a modern Super-Pharoah."

The authoritarian methods of Stalin are too well known to detain us here. One example will suffice. Although he had declared that the decision of the XVth Congress to undertake collectivization would be carried out by persuasion, he resorted to massive coercion. He virtually declared war against the kulaks. Their grain surpluses were confiscated, and their right to hire labor abrogated. Committees of the Poor were organized to "terrorize" and "expropriate" them. Recalcitrant villages were besieged by troops and forced to surrender. It was not unusual for the troops to fire on defiant crowds.

Stalinist Russia was also a highly paternal political system. This is understandable in view of the elitism of Communist parties. Marxist-Leninist theory lays great stress on organization and leadership; in the *Two Tactics* and *What Is to Be Done?*, Lenin stipulates that the party should be the "vanguard" of the proletarian revolution. Stalin made the Russian political system even more elitist by opting for a numerically smaller party. The number of voting delegates in Congress XVIII was 1,567 (representing 1,600,000 members). This meant that membership had dropped by 270,000 since Congress XVII. Defending the trend, Stalin argued that "it is all to the good, for the Party strengthens itself by clearing its ranks of dross. Our Party is now somewhat smaller in membership but on the other hand it is bet-

ter in quality, that is a big achievement."[44] He consulted
the Congress which was theoretically the main decision-
making body somewhat infrequently. For instance, between January, 1934, and March, 1939, there was no
meeting of the Party Congress.

Stalin and his lieutenants reshaped Russia according to their image. They never pretended that their program of industrialization was undertaken in response to
popular demand. For them the industrialization of Russia
was an inescapable responsibility; it was the only way
to save Russia from the "continued beatings she suffered
from falling behind, for her backwardness." There was
no question of shrinking from the responsibility even if
it was unpalatable to the Russian masses: "We are
fifty or a hundred years behind the advanced countries.
We must make good this distance in ten years or they
crush us."[45]

The political system of Russia under Stalin was
highly consensual. It was virtually impossible for a counter-elite to emerge. The Communist party included (and
still does) all citizens of the Soviet Union who possess
"any significant measures of power, privilege, or distinction."[46] With uncanny skill, Stalin's formidable in-
telligence agency took care of people (especially influential people) who were unfavorably disposed towards
the regime; fear of the colossal power of Stalin and his
reputed ruthlessness kept party members compliant;
Communism gave them a common ideological orientation. In his biography of Stalin, Isaac Deutscher relates
an incident which illustrates how completely the mem-

---

[44]Quoted by Frederick L. Schuman, *Russia since 1917* (New York:
Alfred A. Knopf, Inc., 1957) , p. 244.

[45]Joseph Stalin, *Problems of Leninism* (Moscow, 1946) , p. 356.

[46]Frederick C. Barghoorn, "The U.S.S.R.: Monolithic Controls at
Home and Abroad," in Neumann (ed.) , *op. cit.*, p. 220.

bers of the Communist party caucus were controlled by the party. Frunze, Trotsky's successor in the Commissariat of War, had fallen ill in November, 1925. Some of his physicians suggested that he undergo a surgical operation; others objected that he was too weak to survive it. The Politburo promptly decided the issue and ordered the reluctant Frunze to submit to an operation. He obeyed and died during the operation.[47] No sphere of life, however private, was beyond the party's control.

From what has been said so far, it is quite clear that the political system of Stalinist Russia was not highly identific. However, some compensating factors were operative. First, the impressive observable changes that the Communist party elite accomplished in a relatively short time enhanced the prestige and legitimacy of the Stalinist regime. Second, the unifying influence of Marxist-Leninist ideology helped to reduce the mutual alienation of the political class and the ruled. Third, the Stalin regime tried to give the illusion of popular participation. The Stalin Constitution with its promise of popular elections and of judicial bodies and parliaments responsible to the electorate was a step in this direction. Fourth, policies such as the liquidation of the kulaks were supported by a substantial number of people with considerable enthusiasm. The party, the police, and the administrators could not have carried out collectivization so successfully without some support from the rural population. It is clear that the party caucus appreciated this. When Congress XV decreed collectivization in December, 1927, it also directed that 25 percent of the grain surplus seized from the kulaks be offered to the peasants. Stalin found support in the desti-

---

[47]Isaac Deutscher, *Stalin, A Political Biography* (New York: Vintage Books, 1960) , p. 305.

tute, virtually propertyless muzhiks, bitter victims of the kulaks' exploitation. Duetscher estimates that the muzhiks were between five to eight million strong. In contrast, the numerical strength of the kulaks was roughly between one and a half and two million. However, one must not exaggerate the popularity of Stalin's agrarian policies. There were between 15 to 18 million farmers who were neither as wealthy as the kulaks nor as destitute as the muzhiks.[48] It appears that the bulk of this element of the agrarian population was opposed to collectivization.

The Russian experience is particularly instructive because it brings into clearer relief the relation between authoritarianism and the capacity to effect social change and to maintain political stability. In Stalinist Russia a thoroughgoing authoritarianism speeded industrialization by making it possible to avoid lengthy debates and negotiations on policy goals and instruments. Stalin was a rather reluctant reformer until about 1929 when his personal dictatorship was firmly established; collectivization did not go into full swing until the spring of 1929. Authoritarianism made it possible for Stalin to keep the political system consensual; hence, the prospects of political stability were improved. Stalin's determined use of coercive force prevented those whom his policies alienated from expressing their resentment in politically disintegrative behavior; it ensured that no opponent of significant influence survived to challenge the regime. Authoritarianism made it possible to counteract the politically destabilizing effects of the redistribution of power caused by wholesale societal change.

In the final analysis, the Russian experience suggests that a blending of the authoritarian and identific

---

[48]*Ibid.*, pp. 324–25.

elements is in some respects more efficient than exclusive reliance on extreme authoritarianism. Excessive authoritarianism cost Russia dearly. To begin with, it led to unspeakable human suffering and to considerable loss of life. In addition, the resistance that it generated led to a waste of economic resources. Many kulaks burnt both their own farms and the property of the collectives. Some of them slaughtered their livestock and created a desperate shortage of supply. Between 1928 and 1933 the number of horses in the Soviet Union declined from 30,000,000 to less than 15,000,000; sheep from 147,-000,000 to 50,000,000; hogs from 20,000,000 to 12,000,-000.[49] The opposition to collectivization was so determined and its cost in human terms so high that for once, the iron Boss bent a little. On March 2, 1930, in his "Dizziness-with-Success" speech he called for an end to the violence. The pace of collectivization slackened, and in the next three years only 10 percent more of all farm land was collectivized.

The new state that relied exclusively on authoritarianism may well be courting disaster. In Russia the state was well-established; its legitimacy was in no doubt. The political class was backed by a powerful political formula. It also commanded an efficient bureaucracy and a very effective secret police, backed by modern communications techniques. As was pointed out before, these facilities helped minimize open hostility to the regime. The new state hardly boasts such facilities.

The experience of nation-building in Yugoslavia is another interesting commentary on the theory advanced here. The problem of political integration in Yugoslavia was at least as formidable as those of the new states of Africa. Five major national (ethnic) groups—

---

[49]Schuman, *Soviet Politics: At Home and Abroad,* pp. 215 ff.

Serbs, Croats, Slovenes, Macedonians and Montene-
grins—formed the bulk of the population. In addition,
there were many minor ethnic groups, Albanians, Mag-
yars, Turks, Slovaks, Gypsies, Germans, Vlachs, Ruthe-
nians, Italians, Czechs, Bulgars, Russians, Jews, and
Rumanians. The erosion of ethnic particularism was
made more difficult by the fact that each of the national
groups was concentrated in one geographical area. Thus
according to the 1953 census, the Republic of Serbia
was 74.3 percent Serb. In Croatia, 79.8 percent of the
population was Croat, and in Slovenia, 96.5 percent of
the population was Slovenian. Montenegro was 86.4
percent Montenegrin, and Macedonia was 66 percent
Macedonian.

The malintegration of Yugoslavia was compounded
by religious and linguistic differences. Yugoslavia was
an incongruous mixture of religious groups: Orthodox
Churchmen, Roman Catholics, Protestants, and Mos-
lems. In some areas religious differences reinforced ethnic differences. For instance, Serbs were predominantly
Orthodox, while Croats were predominantly Roman
Catholic. The four major languages, Serbian, Croatian,
Slovenian, and Macedonian, are somewhat related.[50] But
there was nothing that could be called an official language.

Such was the rivalry between the ethnic groups—
especially between Serbs, Croatians, and Slovenes—that
when the country now known as Yugoslavia was created,
in October, 1918, it was called the Kingdom of Serbs,
Croats, and Slovenes. It was not until October, 1929,
that the country assumed the name Yugoslavia.

The prospects for the survival of the young country were not helped by the fact that it was dominated

---

[50]Serbian and Croatian are so closely related that for practical purposes they are regarded as one language, Serbo-Croatian.

by Serbs. The Serbian hegemony was resented by the other ethnic groups, especially Croats. As a result the country was plagued by political crises. Shortly after the beginning of the German invasion in April, 1941, Yugoslavia rapidly disintegrated.

Modern Yugoslavia is primarily a creation of the Yugoslavia Communist party. The party (then a guerilla organization known as the Partisans) had led the resistance movement. When the Partisans with the help of the red army liberated Belgrade on October 20, 1944, its political arm, the Committee of National Liberation, became the *de facto* ruler of Yugoslavia. It acted quickly to consolidate its power. In the campaign for the Constituent Assembly, the party resorted to strong-arm tactics; their non-Communist rivals were obliged to boycott the election and the Communist Popular Front gained control of the Assembly. The Assembly which met on November 29, 1945, quickly repudiated the monarchy, adopted a new constitution, and declared itself the People's Assembly of the Federal Republic of Yugoslavia.

If we examine the political structure under which the Communist party of Yugoslavia achieved the country's "integrative revolution," we find that it approximates to our paradigm. Tito's Yugoslavia is highly authoritarian. Under the 1946 Constitution, six theoretically autonomous republics were created. However the list of rights and duties ceded to the national government was so long and these rights and duties so crucial that virtually all important decisions were made by the national government.[51] The national government

---

[51] For more on the 1946 Constitution, see Charles P. McVicker, *Titoism: Pattern for International Communism* (New York: St. Martin's Press, 1957), pp. 139–44. Henry Fabré, *Revue du Droit Public et de la Science Politique* (Paris: Librairie General de Droit et de Jurisprudence, 1946), Vol. LXIII, pp. 456–59.

was in turn dominated by Tito and his lieutenants Rankovic, Djilas, Edvard Kardelj, Boris Kidrić, Mose Pijade. Tito was at the same time secretary general of the Communist party, Premier of Yugoslavia, Chairman of the Politburo, President of the People's Front, Marshal of Yugoslavia, and Minister of Defense. The powerful political police OZNA (Odelenji Zasite Naroda or Department of Defense of the People) efficiently dealt with opponents of the party caucus and enforced its wishes. Even after the decentralizing reforms of the early 50's, the political system was still highly authoritarian. While some concession was made to local autonomy, the idea of a one-party system was maintained in its "monolithic purity."[52]

The political structure of Tito's Yugoslavia is also highly consensual. Hoffman and Neal find that "the Communists were themselves an all Yugoslav group in that they drew equally from the various national groups. Although Tito was a Croat, each of the republics had strong representation in both party and government."[53] The 1946 Constitution abated ethnic-religious particularism by making each of the six national groups an autonomous republic and subordinating all of them to a central government in which each of them was well represented. As soon as it came into power, the Communist party moved to liquidate its opponents. Under the pretext of punishing those who had collaborated with the invaders, the party attacked anybody or any institution of influence which it considered hostile to it. "Nazi collaborator" was defined loosely enough to in-

[52]Rankovic quoted by Fred Warner Neal in *Titoism in Action: The Reforms in Yugoslavia after 1948* (Berkeley: University of California Press, 1958), p. 27.

[53]George W. Hoffman and Fred Warner Neal, *Yugoslavia and the New Communism* (New York: Twentieth Century Fund, 1962), p. 83.

clude "persons ranging from Mihajlović and the Cetniks and the Roman Catholic hierarchy of Croatia and Slovenia to pro-Western politicians and businessmen who had in fact demonstrated hostility to the Nazi-Fascists."[54] In the campaign against collaborators, Draza Mihajlović and his attorney, Dragic Joksimović, were executed. Milos Trifunovic, the Prime Minister of the government-in-exile, was imprisoned. So was Dr. Dragoljub Janovic, a member of the Peoples Assembly. On October 11, 1946, Archbishop Stepinac of the Roman Catholic Church was sentenced to 16 years imprisonment; 8 other priests were sentenced to shorter terms. Some priests of the Orthodox Church were imprisoned, and some branches of the church were closed.

The emergence of a counter-elite was prevented by the control of the Communist party caucus over all major institutions and associations. It has already been noted that the leaders of the Communist party caucus were also the most influential men in the government. All the members of the powerful political police OZNA were communists. Djuro Salaj, the leader of the trade-union movement, was also a member of the Executive Committee of the party. A strenuous effort was made to keep the army and its leaders loyal to the regime. This was considered necessary not only because the army represents a major concentration of power but also because after the Soviet-Yugoslav dispute the Soviet government tried to use the Yugoslav army to subvert the Tito regime. Between 1948 and 1952, 90,948 military men were admitted into the party. This raised army membership of the party to 140,193 by the VIth Party Congress. "Indicative of the attention the party paid to the army was the fact that about 650 party courses were

---

[54]*Ibid.*, p. 91.

organized annually for military personnel, in addition
to about a million political lectures and 700,000 political discussion groups."[55]

Because of the elitism of communist theory, communist political societies are invariably paternal. Yugoslavia is no exception. Even during the decentralizing
reforms of the early 50's the party explicitly reaffirmed
its elite character and rejected the idea of turning itself
into a "mass organization."[56]

As in Russia the elitism of the Communist party
of Yugoslavia imposed severe limits on popular participation in government. However, there were compensating factors. The heroic effort of the Partisans to save
Yugoslavia from the humiliation of the Nazi occupation
won them the respect if not the affection of a grateful
people. What is more, the Communist party has worked
hard to make itself acceptable to the common man. One
of the first things that the Communist party did when
it came to power was to enact an agrarian law which
distributed more than 80 percent of the arable land
among peasants and veterans. This land had been confiscated from wealthy landowners, corporations, and
churches. In addition, the party canceled all peasant
debts in late 1945.

Let us now look at some of the "developing countries" of Latin America and Africa in terms of our theory. Perhaps the Latin American country that has ex-
perienced the most revolutionary change is Cuba. What
is the political structural context of this revolutionary
societal change?

Like other communist states, the political structure

55Neal, *op. cit.*, p. 59.
56*Ibid.*, p. 46.

of Cuba is paternal. A manipulated voluntaryism does little to conceal the fact that initiative is concentrated in the hands of Fidel Castro and the Communist party leadership. The political structure of Cuba is also highly authoritarian. Decision-making power is concentrated in the Communist party, which is in turn ruled by Fidel Castro. Of the 87 members of the party's central committee, 55 are leading army officers and nearly all these army members of the committee were members of Fidel Castro's 26th of July Movement. The Army itself is under Raul Castro, Fidel Castro's brother. All eight members of the Politburo are virtually personal appointees of Fidel Castro. Fidel Castro is the First Secretary of the six-man party Secretariat; his brother Raul Castro is the Second Secretary. As Fitzgibbon has pointed out, Castro dominates Cuba so completely that the history of Cuba in the last few years "is the biography of Fidel."[57]

The system is also highly consensual. The regime eliminated most of its most dangerous enemies when in 1959 it executed 557 people in the name of "revolutionary justice." Shortly after the Castro regime came to power in 1959 the opposition to it rapidly disintegrated. The regime's opponents made things easier for it by fleeing the country. Between 1959 and 1962 about 300,000 people left Cuba. In 1965 about 4,000 more left. The exodus of dissidents continues. Internal opposition to the Castro regime has virtually collapsed.

Castro's Cuba is also considerably identific despite the elitism of communist ideology. Survey research has revealed that Castro is perceived as a charismatic leader

[57]Russell Fitzgibbon, "The Revolution Next Door: Cuba," *Annals of the American Academy of Political and Social Sciences*, Vol. CCCXXXIV (March, 1961) , pp. 113–22.

by his people;[58] his reputation as a guerilla leader is legendary. The populistic tone of Castro's politics has helped promote mutual identity between his regime and the masses. His political style and his personal life dramatize his concern for and identity with the Cuban masses. It is characteristic of Castro's political style that one of the first things he did when he came to power was to create the National Institute of Agrarian Reform (INRA) to effect sweeping agrarian reforms that favored the small farmer. "An amazing variety of charges and accusations has been hurled against the Castro regime, to be sure, but graft and corruption are significantly absent among them."[59] Indeed, Castro has come to symbolize the aspirations of the "common man" for a better life, not only in Cuba, but in Latin America as a whole.

According to our theory then, the political structure of Cuba is adequate for undertaking social change with a minimal danger of political instability. The internal threat to the "persistence" of the existing political structure is small. And foreign intrigue is unlikely to accomplish much more than the assassination of Castro.

If we look at the new states of Africa in the light of the theory, we see that they suffer from a low degree of elite-consensus. Despite "unipartyism" intra-elite competition is intense. The governments which were overthrown in Algeria, Nigeria, the Republic of Sudan, the Central African Republic, Congo (Leopoldville), Congo (Brazzaville), Togo, Dahomey, Ghana, and Upper Volta were victims of palace revolts rather than popular upris-

---

[58]On the charismatic appeal of Castro, see Fitzgibbon, *op. cit.*, pp. 114–17; George Blanksten, "Fidel Castro and Latin America," in Morton A. Kaplan (ed.), *The Revolution in World Politics* (New York and London: John Wiley & Sons, Inc., 1962), pp. 113–36; and Lloyd Free, *Attitudes of the Cuban People toward the Castro Regime* (Princeton, N.J.: Institute of International Social Research, 1966).

[59]Blanksten, *op. cit.*, p. 124.

ings. It appears that the main reason why the Nkrumah regime collapsed was because the degree of elite-consensus was low. Nkrumah never won the support of the powerful Ashanti leaders, nor did he succeed in destroying their power. He never won the support of the universities and some men of great influence such as J. B. Danquah and K. Busia. He alienated powerful interests in the Civil Service by trying to politicize it. Finally, he alienated the military by distrusting it, by compelling senior officers to retire prematurely, and by building up the "Chinese" Presidential Guard as a personal army.

A close examination of Nigeria's recent political history is rewarding because Nigeria presents an example of the effects of a low degree of elite-consensus on political stability. There are three major ethnic groups in Nigeria—Hausa, Ibo, and Yoruba. Each of those groups is very conscious of its cultural uniqueness and deeply suspicious of the others. Ethnic particularism is reinforced by the fact that each of these major ethnic groups is concentrated in one geographical area which is also a major political unit. Within the region of each of the three major ethnic groups there are minority ethnic groups fearful of domination by the majority ethnic group. This fear has found political expression in secessionist movements; in the northern region the Yoruba and Tiv areas of the Middle Belt are demanding the creation of a Middle Belt State; in the eastern region the Efiks and Ibibios are demanding a Calabar-Ogoja Rivers State; in the western region, the Edos, Urhobos, western Ibos, and western Ijaws have already succeeded in getting a separate state, the Mid-West State.

Nigeria never developed an all-Nigeria political party. In the late 40's the National Council of Nigeria and the Cameroons (N.C.N.C.) came nearest to being a national party.[60] But it became increasingly identified with the Ibo. The Action Group (A.G.) and the Northern People's Congress (N.P.C.) were from the very beginning tribal parties. The Action Group was, in effect, a politicization of the Yoruba Cultural Organization Egbe Omo Oduduwa; the very name of the N.P.C. (Jam'iyyar Mutanen Arewa) left no doubt that it was a regional party. Nigerian leaders have emphasized and exploited tribalism ruthlessly. Political competition in Nigeria has become a life-and-death struggle between the different tribes.

It is not surprising that during the series of constitutional conferences leading up to the Constitution with which Nigeria achieved independence everyone was preoccupied with the issue of tribal domination. Each of the major political parties favored an arrangement that would ensure its control of its own region. John Mackintosh is right in pointing out that "in many ways the most remarkable feature of the period and process during which it (the Constitution) was framed was the lack of discussion of how it was likely to work in practice and how far the structure would be affected by the activities and outlook of the Nigerian parties and their leaders."[61]

Let us note the salient characteristics of the Independence Constitution. There are a federal government and three regional governments. The federal government has exclusive power over the 48 items of the Exclusive Legislative List. There is also a concurrent list of 26 items. The power of the federal government is concurrent with that of the regional governments in

---

[60]Now the National Council of Nigerian Citizens.
[61]John P. Mackintosh, *Nigerian Government and Politics* (Evanston: Northwestern University Press: 1966), p. 37.

respect to items on this list. But any regional government law inconsistent with a federal government law in regard to any item on this list is invalid. Among the responsibilities of the federal government are interregional trade, mines, minerals, shipping, waterways, aviation, currency, exchange control, banks, excise tax, business corporations, posts and telegrams, and external borrowing. The regional government can legislate on "residual matters," and this includes local government, health, agriculture, education, income tax, and housing. Like the regional legislatures, the federal legislature is bicameral. It consists of a House of Representatives in which representation is on the basis of population and a Senate in which the regions are equally represented. The bulk of the federal government's power lies in the House of Representatives; the Senate's main power consists in holding up "ordinary" (i.e., nonmoney bills) for a maximum period of six months.

This constitutional structure was not changed in any significant way when Nigeria became a republic in 1963. Nnamdi Azikiwe's proposal for an Executive President was rejected and executive powers remain with the Prime Minister.

One of the most striking things about this constitution is the great amount of power that it concentrates in the hands of the federal government. Given the obsessive fear of tribal domination, it is surprising that a constitution that set up a strong federal government that was bound to be dominated by the Hausa-Fulani North was widely accepted even by non-Hausas. It appears that the Constitution was widely supported because it was generally misunderstood.

As yet by 1960, few Nigerian leaders (including the Northerners) appreciated the power potential of the federal government; nor could they see that the federal government was bound to be dominated by the North.[62] For the moment, the political parties were impressed by the elaborate—but practically ineffective—provisions of regional autonomy embodied in the constitution. Each of the three major parties settled down to consolidating its power within its own region. In each region, the opposition was harassed; local government councils that did not support the ruling party were usually dissolved; electoral districts that failed to return the candidates of the ruling party were denied the most elementary social amenities. Within a short time, each region was virtually a one-party state.

It was not long before the Hausa-dominated federal government began to exercise its vast power. The A.G. which was the opposition party in the federal House of Representatives was one of the first victims of the growing confidence of the N.P.C.-dominated federal government. During the A.G. crisis of May, 1962, the federal government suspended the western regional government which was the power base of the A.G. Many A.G. leaders were imprisoned or placed under preventive detention and a caretaker government was appointed to administer the western region. By December, 1962, the A.G. opposition in the House of Representatives had declined to 13 because of federal government pressures.[63] The Prime Minister then declared that the opposition was too small to merit recognition.

While the federal coalition (made up of the N.P.C. and the N.C.N.C.) oppressed the A.G., the coalition was

---

[62]The constitution is such that the party that controls the House of Representatives controls the federal government. Of the 312 seats allocated according to the 1952–53 census, the North got 174 seats; the East, 73; the West, 62; Lagos, 3.

[63]The A.G. had won 75 seats in the federal elections of 1959.

falling apart. As the subordinate role of the N.C.N.C. in the coalition became more evident, the Ibos began to cast round for a way of curbing N.P.C. power. Meanwhile the N.P.C. was growing more arrogant. As the A.G. collapsed, the N.P.C. collected a few "carpet-crossers" which gave it an absolute majority in the House of Representatives. Thus the N.P.C. no longer needed the partnership of the N.C.N.C. And the N.P.C. made this clear in increasingly brusquer ways. By the end of 1962 the divisions between the leaders of the main tribal groups had become so deep and the fear of tribal domination so obsessive that every issue that had the slightest relevance to the distribution of power was the occasion for a life-and-death political struggle.

It is important to illustrate this in some detail. On May 13, 1962, a census was begun, and the results were available in July. But due to alleged irregularities it was agreed that another census was necessary. On February 24, 1964, the Census Board announced the results of the new census. The southern parties (especially N.C.N.C. and the A.G.) had hoped that the new census would lead to a substantial change in the allocation of seats as a result of which N.P.C. power would be reduced. Unfortunately, this expectation was not borne out. Dr. Okpara, the premier of the East and leader of the N.C.N.C., rejected the new census figures and denounced the N.P.C. for rigging the census. N.P.C. leaders resented the suggestion that they were dishonest and retorted angrily. In both the North and the East, feelings ran high. Alhaji Gashash, the Northern Minister of Land and Survey, threatened that Ibos would soon be prevented from owning land in the North. The Kano Native Authority instructed over 2,000 non-Northerners to leave the North within two days. Quite a few other

northern towns including Gusau and Katsina expelled
their Ibo residents. Only the personal intervention of
the Sardauna prevented a mass exodus of Ibos. Meanwhile the Eastern region openly talked of secession. The
Eastern government put out a publication accusing the
N.P.C. of abusing its power by channeling £262 million into the development of the North. Ultimately the
N.C.N.C. was obliged to accept the census figures. But
the crisis brought the country one step nearer disintegration.[64]

If the uncomplicated process of counting heads
caused a fitful crisis, it is hardly surprising that the federal election of 1964 almost destroyed the country. Electoral victory had become so important that the political
parties were inclined to seek it by any means—however
unscrupulous or unconstitutional. In the western region,
the campaigns virtually degenerated into a civil war between the United Nigerian Progressive Grand Alliance
(an alliance of the A.G. and the N.C.N.C.) and the Nigerian National Alliance (an alliance of Akintola's
Nigerian National Democratic Party and the N.P.C.).
Two N.N.A. leaders, Prince Odufunnade and Ogunloye

---

[64]The census crisis is also an interesting commentary on the advis-
ability of undertaking industrialization with a political system that is not substantially consensual. The counting and recounting made necessary not by
technical inefficiency but by political pressures were a waste of resources. There
were so many charges and countercharges of irregularities and so many rival
figures during the controversy that no one knows for certain how many
Nigerians there are and how this population is distributed. And such information is necessary for efficient economic planning.

Another example of the difficulties of industrializing in the context of a
political system with a low elite-consensus is relevant here. The 1962–68
Development Plan contained a proposal for a steel mill. The North wanted
it built at Idah; the East argued for Onitsha; the West proposed Ikare. Because of the weak political position of the West, its claim was easily brushed
aside. As a result of the intransigence of the North and the East, it was
decided that two mills be built, one in Onitsha and the other at Idah. This
was far from being the soundest economic decision. The estimated cost of the
project has since risen from £30 million to over £50 million.

Fakunmoju, were killed. Riots erupted; mobs roamed cities and villages burning cars and houses. The N.N.A.-controlled regional government refused to issue permits for U.P.G.A. campaign meetings and arrested some U.P.G.A. leaders. In Ondo, a U.P.G.A. supporter was killed by the police.

In the North the campaign was equally violent. Alhaji Amino Kano, the leader of the Northern Elements Progressive Union, a minority party opposed to the N.P.C., complained that many of his party candidates had been arbitrarily imprisoned.[65] When Dr. Okpara went to the North on a campaign tour, he was refused entry into Bauchi and Katsina. The newspapers were full of reports about acts of terrorism against U.P.G.A. candidates. Some lawyers who were sent from the South to defend U.P.G.A. supporters were summarily arrested. It was alleged that many candidates had been prevented from campaigning because of intimidation and kidnapping and that in two Sokoto constituencies, Gwadabawa North and Binji-Tangaza-Silame, the two anti-N.N.A. candidates had been killed. In the East there was much less violence. One suspects that this was due to the failure of N.N.A. leaders to make a serious campaign effort in the East rather than to the self-restraint of U.P.G.A. leaders.

Because of the manner in which the campaign was conducted, Dr. Okpara, the leader of the UPGA, demanded that the elections be postponed. The NNA refused and Dr. Okpara decided to boycott the election. After the election, the Governor-General, Nnamdi Azikiwe, refused to invite Alhaji Abubakar Tafawa Balewa, the leader of the NNA parliamentary party, to form a new government on the grounds that the elec-

---

[65]Allegedly 26 of them.

tion had not been properly contested. But then, the NNA would not hear of another election. The political struggle had reached a stalemate. For a few days after the election Nigeria had no government. Eventually Dr. Okpara gave in and accepted the result of the election in those places where the boycott had not been effective. But it was clear that the compromise merely papered over the cracks. In the East the secessionist feeling reached a fever pitch, especially now that the N.P.C. was talking of using the emergency powers of the federal government to crush the Ibo-East in much the same way that the A.G. government of the West had been crushed in 1962.

On the eve of the coup of January 15, 1966, Nigeria was grappling with yet another crisis. This arose from the West regional election of October 11, 1965. Supporters of the A.G. and the N.C.N.C. were convinced that the NNDP had rigged the election. Riots erupted. There was widespread looting, killing, and arson. By December the disturbances were spreading to the Lagos area, and the federal government imposed a two-month ban on public meetings and processions in Lagos. On January 5, 1967, the western region imposed a dusk-to-dawn curfew on several districts in the region. The Ibadan police arrested and detained without charges 25 key personnel of the Nigerian Press, publishers of the A.G. *Nigerian Tribune* and *Irohin,* and the premises of the Nigerian Press were declared a prohibited area to all persons. On January 6, angry A.G. demonstrators retaliated by raiding the premises of the Ibadan office of the *Daily Sketch* (an NNDP publication) and the *Morning Post* (an NNA oriented newspaper). The federal Minister of State for the Police, Alhaji Angulu Ahmad, told the House of Representatives on January

13 that 153 persons had been killed during the disturbances. Some other unofficial sources estimated that as
many as 700 people lost their lives. Whatever the figures, it was evident that by January 15, the day of the
coup, law and order had almost completely broken
down in the western region.

It is unfortunate that after two coups and the slaugh-
ter of over 30,000 Ibos, the power struggle in Nigeria is
still somewhat indecisive. The North has reasserted its
strength and dominance; but the East is still very much
in the competition. To all appearances Nigeria will
continue to be plagued by crises until one of the con-
tending political groups accumulates sufficient power to
cripple its opponents and establish a highly authoritarian political system. An alternative way of increasing
the political stability of Nigeria is to create a power
balance between the main tribal groups; this will greatly
allay the fear of tribal domination and lower the price
of political competition and hence reduce the propensity to employ unconstitutional methods in political
competition.

The Nigerian experience underlines the importance of elite-consensus. In Nigeria, an almost total lack
of any measure of elite-consensus allowed politicians to
exploit tribal differences so ruthlessly that there is virtually no basic trust among the different tribal groups.
The absence of basic trust put political competitors under very heavy pressure to win the struggle for power
because victory was the only guarantee of personal security; this pressure forced them to be very flexible
about their methods of seeking and exercising power.
The flow of exchanges between the different units of
the political system was thus subjected to erratic variations. And this meant political instability.

This survey of historical political systems is too impressionistic to pretend to establish the empirical validity of our theory. It is necessary to study a greater sample of historical societies—and in greater detail—taking care to consider inconvenient facts. It is also necessary to show with greater analytic rigor the significance of each of the four key variables of the theory in every historical political system used as a case study.

All the same, this hasty incursion into political history has not been entirely useless because it has helped clarify the key concepts of the theory. For instance, the kind of empirical evidence adduced to show that a particular historical political system was paternal helps to make more explicit the kind of data that the concept "paternal" subsumes. The testability of the theory has been increased not only by this clarificatory process but also by the fact that in the course of this survey, I have offered in terms of the theory, "falsifiable" propositions about the experience of historical political systems.

Political reality is complex. The capacity of the political system to undertake social mobilization and to withstand the disintegrative impact of rapid social change depends on more factors than our four variables encompass. Hopefully, the theory advanced here has shed some light on the conditions of political integration, social mobilization, and political stability and has supplied a means for a systematic exploration of the relation between the three phenomena.

Selected Bibliography

ADORNO, T. W. *et al. The Authoritarian Personality.* New York: Harper & Bros., 1950.

AKE, CLAUDE. "Pan-Africanism and African Governments," *The Review of Politics,* Vol. XXVII, No. 4 (October, 1965), pp. 532–42.

———. "Political Integration and Political Stability: A Hypothesis," *World Politics,* Vol. XIX, No. 3 (April, 1967), pp. 486–99.

ALLARDT, ERIC, AND YRJO, LITTUNEN (eds.). *Cleavages, Ideologies and Party Systems: Contributions to Comparative Political Sociology.* Transactions of the Westermarck Society, Vol. X. Helsinki, 1964.

ALMOND, GABRIEL, AND COLEMAN, JAMES (eds.). *The Politics of Developing Areas.* Princeton, N.J.: Princeton University Press, 1960.

ANGELL, ROBERT. *The Integration of American Society.* New York: McGraw-Hill Book Co., Inc., 1941.

APTER, DAVID. *Ghana in Transition.* New York: Atheneum Publishers, 1963.

———. *The Politics of Modernization.* Chicago: The University of Chicago Press, 1965.

———. "Political Democracy in the Gold Coast," in *Africa in the Modern World* (ed. C. STILLMAN). Chicago: University of Chicago Press, 1955.

———. "The Role of Traditionalism in the Political Modernization of Ghana and Uganda," *World Politics,* Vol. XIII (October, 1960), pp. 45–68.

ASHFORD, DOUGLAS E. *The Elusiveness of Power: The African Sin-*

gle-Party State. Cornell Research Papers in International Studies, No. III. Ithaca, N.Y., 1965.

AYER, A. J. *Language, Truth and Logic.* 2d ed. London: V. Gollanancz, 1946.

BARRINGER, HERBERT R.; BLANKSTEN, GEORGE I.; AND MACK, RAYMOND W. (eds.). *Social Change in Developing Areas.* Cambridge, Mass.: Schenkman Publishing Co., 1965.

BENDIX, REINHARD. *Nation-Building and Citizenship.* New York: John Wiley & Sons, Inc., 1964.

BINDER, LEONARD. *Iran: Political Development in a Changing Society.* Berkeley: University of California Press, 1962.

——. "National Integration and Political Development," *American Political Science Review,* Vol. LVII, No. 3 (September, 1964), pp. 622–63.

BONNAFE, P., AND CARTRY, M. "Les Ideologies Politiques des Pays en Voie de Developpement," *Revue Francaise de Science Politique,* Vol. XII (June, 1962), pp. 417–25.

BRECHT, ARNOLD. *Political Theory: The Foundations of Twentieth Century Political Thought.* Princeton, N.J.: Princeton University Press, 1959.

BUTWELL, RICHARD. "Individual and Collective Identity in Nation Building," *World Politics,* Vol. XV, No. 3 (April, 1963), pp. 488–94.

CARTER, GWENDOLEN (ed.). *African One-Party States.* Ithaca, N.Y.: Cornell University Press, 1962.

COLEMAN, JAMES. *Nigeria: Background to Nationalism.* Berkeley and Los Angeles: University of California Press, 1958.

——. "The Problem of Political Integration in Emergent Africa," *Western Political Quarterly,* Vol. VIII, No. 1 (March, 1955), pp. 44–58.

——. "The Character and Viability of African Political Systems," in *The United States and Africa.* Rev. ed. New York: American Assembly, 1963.

——. "The Emergence of African Political Parties," in *Africa Today* (ed. C. GROVE HAINES), pp. 225–55. Baltimore: Johns Hopkins Press, 1955.

—— AND ROSBERG, CARL. *Political Parties and National Inte-*

gration in Tropical Africa. Berkeley and Los Angeles: University of California Press, 1966.

DAHL, ROBERT. "A Critique of the Ruling Elite Model," *American Political Science Review,* Vol. LII, No. 2 (June, 1958), pp. 463–69.

———. *Modern Political Analysis.* Englewood Cliffs, N.J.: Prentice-Hall, Inc., 1963.

DAVIES, JAMES. "Charisma in the 1952 Campaign," *American Political Science Review,* Vol. XLVIII (1954), pp. 1083–1102.

DEUTSCH, KARL. *The Nerves of Government: Models of Political Communication and Control.* New York: Free Press of Glencoe, Inc., 1963.

———. *Nationalism and Social Communication: An Inquiry into the Foundations of Nationality.* New York: M.I.T. and John Wiley & Sons, Inc., 1953.

——— (ed.), *Nation-Building.* New York: Atherton Press, 1963.

——— et al. *Political Community and the North Atlantic Area: International Organization in the Light of Historical Experience.* Princeton, N.J.: Princeton University Press, 1957.

———. "Social Mobilization and Political Development," *American Political Science Review,* Vol. LV (September, 1961), pp. 493–514.

———. "The Growth of Nations: Some Recurrent Patterns of Political and Social Integration," *World Politics,* Vol. V, No. 2 (January, 1953), pp. 168–95.

———. "Communication Theory and Political Integration," in *The Integration of Political Communities* (eds. P. JACOB AND J. TOSCANO), pp. 46–74. New York: J. B. Lippincott Co., 1964.

———. "The Price of Integration," in *The Integration of Political Communities* (eds. P. JACOB AND J. TOSCANO), pp. 143–78. New York: J. B. Lippincott Co., 1964.

DUDLEY, B. J. "Federalism and the Balance of Political Power in Nigeria," *Journal of Commonwealth Political Studies,* Vol. IV, No. 1 (March, 1966), pp. 16–29.

DURKHEIM, EMILE. *The Division of Labor in Society.* Trans. GEORGE SIMPSON. New York: The Macmillan Co., 1933.

EISENSTADT, S. N. "Processes of Modernization and of Urban

and Industrial Transition under Conditions of Structural Duality," *Social Science Information,* Vol. IV, No. 1 (March, 1965).

————. "Social Change and Modernization in African Societies South of the Sahara," *Cahiers d'Etudes Africaines,* Vol. V, No. 3 (1965), pp. 453–71.

————. "Transformation of Social, Political and Cultural Orders in Modernization," *American Sociological Review,* Vol. X (October, 1965), pp. 549–64.

EMERSON, R. "Nationalism and Political Development," *Journal of Politics,* Vol. XXII (February, 1960), pp. 3–28.

————. *Political Modernization: The Single-Party System.* University of Denver Monograph Series in World Affairs, No. 1. Denver, 1964.

————. *From Empire to Nation: The Rise of Self-Assertion of Asian and African People.* Cambridge, Mass.: Harvard University Press, 1960.

ERIKSON, E. *Young Man Luther: A Study in Psychoanalysis and History.* New York: W. W. Norton & Co., Inc., 1958.

————. "The Problem of Ego Identity," *Journal of the American Psycholanalytic Association,* Vol. IV (January, 1956), pp. 56–121.

ETZIONI, AMITAI. "A Paradigm for the Study of Political Unification," *World Politics,* Vol. XV (October, 1962), pp. 44–74.

FALLARS, LLOYD. "Ideology and Culture in Uganda Nationalism," *American Anthropologist,* Vol. LXIII (August, 1961), pp. 677–88.

FRIEDRICH, CARL. "Political Leadership and the Problem of Charismatic Power," *Journal of Politics,* Vol. XXIII, No. 1 (February, 1961), pp. 3–24.

FREUD, SIGMUND. *Group Psychology and the Analysis of the Ego.* Trans. JAMES STRACHEY. New York: Liveright Publishing Co., 1959.

————. *Civilization and Its Discontents.* Trans. JOAN RIVIERE. London: Hogarth Press, 1953.

GITTEL, MARILYN. "A Topology of Power for Measuring Social

Change," *American Behavioral Scientist,* Vol. IX, No. 8 (April, 1966), pp. 23–28.

GEERTZ, CLIFFORD. "The Integrative Revolution: Primordial Loyalties and Civil Politics in the New States," in *Old Societies and New States: The Quest for Modernity in Asia and Africa* (ed. CLIFFORD GEERTZ). New York: Free Press of Glencoe, Inc., 1963.

HAAS, ERNST B. *The Uniting of Europe: Political, Social and Economic Forces.* Stanford, Calif.: Stanford University Press, 1958.

HAGEN, EVERETT. *On the Theory of Social Change.* Homewood, Ill.: The Dorsey Press, Inc., 1962.

HALPERN, MANFRED. "The Rate and Costs of Political Development," *Annals of the American Academy,* Vol. CCCLVIII (March, 1965), pp. 20–28.

HARRIS, RICHARD. "Nigeria! Crisis and Compromise," *Africa Report,* Vol. X, No. 3 (March, 1965), pp. 25–31.

HAYES, CARLTON J. *Essays in Nationalism.* New York: The Macmillan Co., 1926.

HODGKIN, T. *African Political Parties.* Baltimore: Penguin Books, 1961.

———. *Nationalism in Colonial Africa.* London: Frederick Muller, 1956.

HONDMON, M. "The Sentiments of Nationalism," *Political Science Quarterly,* Vol. XXXVI, pp. 104–22.

HUNTINGTON, SAMUEL P. "Political Development and Political Decay," *World Politics,* Vol. XVII, No. 3 (April, 1965), pp. 386–430.

———. "Political Modernization: America vs. Europe," *World Politics* (April, 1966), pp. 378–414.

JACOB, P. "The Influence of Values in Political Integration," in *The Integration of Political Communities* (eds. P. JACOB AND J. TOSCANO). New York: J. B. Lippincott Co., 1964.

JACOB, P., AND TUENE, H. "The Integrative Process: Guidelines for Analysis of the Bases of Political Community," in *The Integration of Political Communities* (eds. P. JACOB AND J. TOSCANO), pp. 1–45. New York: J. B. Lippincott Co., 1964.

JANOWITZ, MORRIS. *The Military in the Political Development of New Nations.* Chicago: University of Chicago Press, 1964.

JOHNSON, CHALMORS. *Revolutionary Change.* Boston and Toronto: Little Brown & Co., 1966.

JOHNSON, J. (ed.). *The Role of the Military in Underdeveloped Countries.* Princeton, N.J.: Princeton University Press, 1962.

KAHIN, G. (ed.). *Government and Politics in South-East Asia.* Ithaca, N.Y.: Cornell University Press, 1959.

KAPLAN, A., AND LASSWELL, H. *Power and Society.* New Haven, Conn.: Yale University Press, 1950.

KAUTSKY, JOHN (ed.). *Political Change in Underdeveloped Countries: Nationalism and Communism.* New York: John Wiley & Sons, Inc., 1962.

KILSON, MARTIN. "Authoritarianism and Single-Party Tendencies in African Politics," *World Politics,* Vol. XV, No. 2 (January, 1963), pp. 262–94.

KORNHAUSER, WILLIAM. *The Politics of Mass Society.* New York: Free Press of Glencoe, Inc., 1959.

LANE, ROBERT. *Political Ideology: Why the American Common Man Believes What He Does.* New York: Free Press of Glencoe, Inc., 1962.

LASSWELL, HAROLD. "The Psychology of Hitlerism," *Political Quarterly,* Vol. IV (1933), pp. 373–84.

LEMARCHAND, RENÉ. "L'Influence des Systèms Traditionnels sur L'Évolution politique du Rwanda et du Burundi," *Revue de L'Institut de Sociologie* (1962), pp. 333–57.

LEVY, MARION, JR. "Patterns (Structures) of Modernization and Political Development," *Annals of the American Academy,* Vol. CCCLVIII (March, 1965), pp. 29–40.

LEWIS, W. H. (ed.). *French-Speaking West Africa: The Search for Identity.* New York: Walker & Company, 1965.

LIPSET, SEYMOUR M. *The First New Nation: The United States in Historical and Comparative Perspective.* New York: Basic Books Publishing Co., 1963.

MACHIAVELLI, NICCOLÒ. *The Prince and the Discourses.* With an introduction by MAX LERNER. New York: The Modern Library, 1940.

MANN, THOMAS C. "Disparities in Progress among Nations," *Annals of the American Academy,* Vol. CCCLX (July, 1965), pp. 63–67.

MARVICK, DWAINE (ed.). *Political Decision-Makers.* New York: Free Press of Glencoe, Inc., 1961.

McALISTER, LYLE N. "Changing Concepts of the Role of the Military in Latin America," *Annals of the American Academy,* Vol. CCCLX (July, 1965), pp. 85–98.

MERELMAN, RICHARD M. "Learning and Legitimacy," *American Political Science Review,* Vol. LX, No. 3 (September, 1966), pp. 548–61.

MICAUD, D. *Tunisia: The Politics of Modernization.* New York: Frederick A. Praeger, Inc., 1964.

MICHELS, ROBERT. *First Lectures in Political Sociology.* Trans. ALFRED DE GRAZIA. Minneapolis: University of Minnesota Press, 1949.

MOORE. C. H. "The National Party: A Tentative Model," in *Public Policy.* Cambridge, Mass.: Harvard University Press, 1960.

MOSCA, GAETANO. *The Ruling Class (Elementi di Scienza Politica).* Trans. H. D. KAHN. New York: McGraw-Hill Book Co., Inc., 1939.

MOSKOS, CHARLES C., JR., AND WENDELL BELL. "Cultural Unity and Diversity in New States," *Teachers College Record,* Vol. LXVI, No. 3 (May, 1965), pp. 670–94.

NEEDLER, MARTIN C. "Political Development and Military Intervention in Latin America," *American Political Science Review,* Vol. LX, No. 3 (September, 1966), pp. 616–23.

NEUMANN, FRANZ. *The Democratic and the Authoritarian State: Essays in Political and Legal Theory* (ed. Herbert Marcuse). New York: Free Press of Glencoe, Inc., 1957.

NKRUMAH, KWAME. *I Speak of Freedom.* New York: Frederick A. Praeger, Inc., 1962.

OBSE, D., AND JESSNER, L. "The Psychodynamics of Leadership," in *Excellence and Leadership in a Democracy* (eds. GRAUBARD AND HOLTON). New York: Columbia University Press, 1962.

O'CONNELL, JAMES. "The Concept of Modernization," *South Atlantic Quarterly,* Vol. LXIV, No. 4 (Autumn, 1965), pp. 549–64.

158 *A Theory of Political Integration*

OPPENHEIM, FELIX. "In Defense of Relativism," *The Western Political Quarterly,* Vol. VIII, No. 3 (September, 1955), pp. 441–47.

PARSONS, TALCOTT. "Authority, Legitimation and Political Action," in *Authority* (ed. CARL FRIEDRICH). Cambridge, Mass.: Harvard University Press, 1958.

———. *The Structure of Social Action.* London and New York: McGraw-Hill Book Co., Inc., 1937.

PAYNE, JAMES. "Peru: The Politics of Structured Violence," *Journal of Politics,* Vol. XXVII, No. 2 (May, 1965), pp. 362–74.

PENNOCK, J. ROLAND. "Political Development, Political Systems and Political Goods," *World Politics,* Vol. XVIII, No. 3 (April, 1966), pp. 415–34.

POLK, WILLIAM R. "The Nature of Modernization: The Middle East & North America," *Foreign Affairs,* Vol. XLIV, No. 1 (October, 1965), pp. 100–110.

PYE, LUCIAN. "The Concept of Political Development," *Annals of the American Academy,* Vol. CCCLVIII (March, 1965), pp. 1–13.

———. "Personal Identity and Political Ideology," in *Political Decision-Makers* (ed. DWAINE MARVICK). New York: Free Press of Glencoe, Inc., 1961.

———. *Politics, Personality and Nation-Building: Burma's Search for Identity.* New Haven: Yale University Press, 1962.

RIEMER, NEAL. "Democratic Theory and the New States: The Dilemma of Transition," *Bucknell Review,* Vol. XIII, No. 1 (March, 1965), pp. 1–16.

RIGA, PETER. "Modernization and Revolutionary Change," *World Justice,* Vol. VII, No. 3 (March, 1966), pp. 336–67.

RUNCIMAN, W. G. "Charismatic Legitimacy and One-Party Rule in Ghana," *Archives Europeennes de Sociologie,* Vol. IV, No. 1 (1963), pp. 148–65.

SCHACHTER, RUTH. "Single-Party Systems in West Africa," *American Political Science Review,* Vol. LV, No. 2 (June, 1961), pp. 294–307.

SHILS, EDWARD. "The Concentration and Dispersion of Charisma: Their Bearing on Economic Policy in Underdeveloped Countries," *World Politics,* Vol. XI, No. 1 (October, 1958), pp. 1–19.

————. "Charisma, Order and Status," *American Sociological Review*, Vol. XXX, No. 2 (April, 1965), pp. 199–213.

————. "On the Comparative Study of the New States," in *Old Societies and New States* (ed. CLIFFORD GEERTZ). New York: Free Press of Glencoe, Inc., 1963.

————. "The Intellectuals in the Political Development of the New States," *World Politics*, Vol. XII (April, 1960), pp. 329–68.

————. "Political Development in the New States," *Comparative Studies in Society and History*, Vol. II (1960), pp. 265–97, 397–411.

SIEGAL, BERNARD. "Some Recent Developments in Studies of Social and Cultural Change," *Annals of the American Academy*, Vol. CCCLVIII (January, 1966), pp. 137–53.

SIGMUND, PAUL (ed.). *The Ideologies of Developing Countries*. New York: Frederick A. Præger, Inc., 1963.

SIMMEL, GEORGE. *Conflict: The Web of Group Affiliation*. Trans. K. WOLFF AND R. BENDIX. New York: Free Press of Glencoe, Inc., 1964.

SNOW, PETER G. "A Scalogram Analysis of Political Development," *American Behavioral Scientist*, Vol. IX, No. 7 (March, 1966), pp. 33–36.

SUTTON, FRANCIS. "Authority and Authoritarianism in the New Africa," *Journal of International Affairs*, Vol. XV, No. 1 (1961), pp. 7–17.

TIRYAKIAN, EDWARD. "African Political Development," *World Politics*, Vol. XIV (July, 1962), pp. 700–712.

TORRES, J. A. "The Political Ideology of Guided Democracy," *Review of Politics*, Vol. XXV (January, 1963), pp. 34–63.

TUCKER, ROBERT C. "The Dictator and Totalitarianism," *World Politics*, Vol. XVII, No. 4 (July, 1965), pp. 553–83.

ULAM, A. HALUK, AND TACHU, FRANK. "Turkish Politics: The Attempt to Reconcile Rapid Modernization with Democracy," *Middle East Journal*, Vol. XIX, No. 2 (Spring, 1965), pp. 153–68.

VORYS, KARL VON. "Toward a Concept of Political Development," *Annals of the American Academy*, Vol. CCCLVIII (March, 1965), pp. 14–19.

WALLERSTEIN, IMMANUEL. "Elites in French-Speaking West Africa: The Social Basis of Ideas," *Journal of Modern African Studies,* Vol. III, No. 1 (May, 1965), pp. 1–34.

———. "Ethnicity and National Integration in West Africa," *Cahiers d'Etudes Africaines,* No. 3 (October, 1960), pp. 129–39.

———. "The Political Ideology of the P.D.G.," *Présence Africaine* (English ed.), Vol. XII (First Quarter, 1962), pp. 30–41.

———. *Africa: The Politics of Independence.* New York: Vintage Books, 1961.

WALTON, RICHARD E. "Two Strategies of Social Change and Their Dilemmas," *Journal of Applied Behavioral Science,* Vol. I, No. 2 (April–June, 1965), pp. 167–79.

WEBER, MAX. *The Theory of Social and Economic Organization.* Trans. T. PARSONS AND A. M. HENDERSON. New York: Free Press of Glencoe, Inc., 1964.

WEINER, MYRON. "Political Integration and Political Development," *Annals of the American Academy,* Vol. CCCLVIII (March, 1965), pp. 52–64.

——— (ed.). *Modernization: The Dynamics of Growth.* New York: Basic Books Publishing Co., 1966.

WILLIAMS, OLIVER. "Urban Differentiation and Political Integration." Paper delivered at the American Political Science Association Annual Meeting, September 5–8, 1962.

WILNER, ANN, AND WILNER, DOROTHY. "The Rise and Role of Charismatic Leaders," *Annals of the American Academy,* Vol. CCCLVIII (March, 1965), pp. 77–88.

WRIGGINS, W. H. "Impediments to Unity in the New States: The Case of Ceylon," *American Political Science Review,* Vol. LV, No. 2 (June, 1961), pp. 313–20.

ZARTMAN, I. WILLIAM. *Government and Politics in Northern Africa.* New York: Frederick A. Praeger, Inc., 1963.

ZOLBERG, ARISTIDE. "Effets de la Structure d'un Parti Politique sur l'Integration Nationale," *Cahiers d'Etudes Africaines,* No. 3 (October, 1960), pp. 140–49.

———. "Mass Parties and National Integration: The Case of the Ivory Coast," *Journal of Politics,* Vol. XXV, No. 1 (February, 1963), pp. 36–48.

Index

This book has been set in 12 point Baskerville, leaded 3 points, and 11 point Baskerville, leaded 2 points. Chapter numbers are in 14 point Bodoni Bold Italic and chapter titles are in 24 point Bodoni Bold. The size of the type page is 24 by 44½ picas.